To Gerald & Peg:

In appreciation of a
new acquaintance ship
on our trip to Ireland.

Lawrence M. Enright
9-30-'83

LAWRENCE M. BRINGS,
Book Publisher

Men of Achievement Series

LAWRENCE M. BRINGS,

Book Publisher

By

GLADYS ZEHNPFENNIG

Publishers

T. S. DENISON & COMPANY, INC.

Minneapolis

 T. S. DENISON & COMPANY, INC.

Standard Book Number: 513-01309-1
Library of Congress Card Number: 73-77194
Printed in the United States of America
by The Brings Press
Copyright © MCMLXXIII by T. S. Denison & Co., Inc.
Minneapolis, Minn. 55437

A DEDICATION

To the many individuals who contributed in various ways to the accomplishments of the subject of this biography.

Contents

Chapter One

Roots in the Soil

The influence of Lawrence M. Brings stretches far and wide in educational circles. Textbooks that his company has published are in daily service on teachers' desks from Maine to California. In the same classrooms, students are bending over individual workbooks published by T. S. Denison & Company.

In school and public libraries, young people journey to exotic, faraway places in Denison books —and dream of their own future world travels. Readers of all ages seek inspiration in *We Believe in Prayer* and other devotional books that Lawrence Brings considers vitally essential in our hectic modern age. Many booklovers keep searching for a sense of direction—with clues to the development of their own special talents—in the T. S. Denison "Men of Achievement" series, the "Famous American Leaders" series, and the "Lives of Great Americans" series.

This book will contain clues to the development of a publisher's talents, a story with more drama and humor than many fictional plots. Lawrence Mar-

tin Brings, the editor and publisher of the "Men of
Achievement" biographical series and a multitude
of educational books and amateur plays, is a man of
achievement in his own right.

As with all biographies of this type, we must ask
ourselves, "Why is Lawrence M. Brings a man of
special consequence?" After years of association with
him, most of his authors can appreciate the dramatic
contradictions that have set him apart—as a person,
a publisher, and a highly articulate gentleman who
could have been a rousing success in politics or the
theater.

Why would an author want to write a biography
about her publisher? Publishers are supposed to be
the natural enemies of authors. They are considered
frugal about royalties and indifferent to the blood-
sweating agony of creative genius. Even Thomas
Wolfe became disillusioned with Maxwell Perkins.

Lawrence M. Brings has remained on amicable
terms with scores of authors and playwrights and
has even managed to grin at the one who enjoyed
teasing him—effervescent Truly Trousdale Latchaw
—daughter in spirit and personality of the touring
theatrical Trousdales — who was assistant editor
with Lawrence Brings in producing a handsome
historical volume called *Minnesota Heritage*. Truly
sometimes tossed this reproachful quote at him:
"You know publishers drink champagne from authors' skulls!" Since Mr. Brings is not the type to
sit around sipping champagne, it was twice as funny.

Lawrence M. Brings is a careful businessman,
with some peculiar differences. He has worked ex-

tremely hard to build his company—but he has also devoted immeasurable time and personal energy to the promotion of civic and humanitarian projects. Most notably, he has helped to build a handsome Foundation fund for Central Lutheran Church in Minneapolis where he served as Superintendent of the Sunday school from 1923 to 1938 and for over thirty years as a member of the Board of Trustees, officiating as chairman for twenty-six years. If he had directed all his aggressive efforts and talents toward enriching himself—instead of laboring diligently to build a "spiritual cathedral" for an expanding urban congregation—and other charitable activities—Lawrence Brings might well be a rich man today.

The Minneapolis publisher has chosen to be "different" in an even more astonishing way. In this pornographic age, the surest path to literary fame and fortune is the "lewdity and nudity trail"—but not at T. S. Denison! L. M. Brings has furnished a marketplace for authors who love to express themselves eloquently, with dignity, sprightliness and humor. They are never prudish when you talk to them, but vulgarity seems alien to their vocabularies.

At a time when it is intellectually stylish for publishers to lick their chops over obscene manuscripts—and urge authors to insert even more sex for the sake of sales—LMB's philosophy is an editorial phenomenon. There is a patriotic aspect to his devotion to clean literature. He is convinced that a country that is obsessed with sex is not a healthy country. Immorality is an obvious form of extremism, joining all the others to claw with dirty finger-nails at the fabric of American society.

If Lawrence M. Brings wanted to "make a million" by publishing literature that appeals to the baser human emotions, he has had enough opportunities. He grins wryly when he mentions some smutty masterpieces that have been submitted to him, by "big name authors" in several instances. He answered with flat rejections, conveying the impression that he couldn't wait to get those manuscripts out of the building. On the other hand, an "inoffensive" manuscript does not guarantee acceptance either, if it is amateurish and poorly written, as well as unsuitable for the company's market.

If you pass through the east door of the new T. S. Denison plant, situated on ten acres, in the middle of the morning, you are likely to see a stack of freshly delivered mail. There are manuscript-sized packages of various thicknesses, and you think of the hopes and dreams of authorship that are wrapped up in them, the burning of the midnight oil, the creative faith that filled those pages. Will the verdict be heartbreak, or the glory of a published book? If you are an author, you pause for a wistful moment, remembering.

Whether he sits in an office in Manhattan or Minneapolis, a publisher is a powerful man. His is the gesture of destiny—thumbs up or thumbs down —that will decide who will be the dispensers of knowledge and entertainment. Publishers are eminent, distinguished figures, with more invisible authority than the bottomside of an iceberg. When they receive rejection slips, some writers think that publishers are as coldhearted as icebergs.

Most of the gentlemen in the "Men of Achievement" series started their successful lives with few material advantages, and Lawrence Brings certainly was "underprivileged" by modern standards. Talk about humble beginnings! Lawrence's future father, Lee Brings, was allowed to celebrate his marriage to Bertha Haugen by keeping the money he made on sales at the vegetable market—two whole dollars —on his wedding day. Lee had been living with his father on White Bear Avenue in St. Paul, Minnesota, earning his "keep" by taking care of the truck farm on the home place.

Before he retired, the paternal grandfather had operated a cooperage business — manufacturing wooden barrels—in St. Paul after the Civil War. The cooperage business is a lost art. So is the strict domination of the father as "the head of the family." After their marriage, Lee kept working in the truck garden and Bertha took care of the housework under the paternal roof, but they were financially dependent on the father who held the purse strings. In those days, it was a fairly normal arrangement.

The young couple's first child, Lawrence Martin Brings, was born on September 29, 1897, in his grandfather's house. Two years later, the first daughter was born, and again, in 1901, the second daughter arrived. In all cases, a midwife was in attendance.

Lawrence's mother often described a blood-curdling performance that her two-year-old son staged, during her second confinement in the big double bed in the upstairs bedroom. Somehow the toddler managed to climb to the top of the high, narrow footboard at the end of the bedstead and stand upright, balancing himself precariously. Then he proceeded to walk along the narrow perch, putting one little foot ahead of the other, just like a high-wire acrobat in a circus. His poor mother held her breath, feeling terrified. She didn't dare to call for help, because the child might become alarmed and topple to the hard floor. Finally little Larry scrambled safely down, without cracking his head.

That was probably the first of Larry Brings' "impossible feats." He demonstrated, early in life, that he dared to take imaginative chances on the spur of the moment, with little regard for the consequences.

One day, when little Larry was almost five years old, his grandfather came home and announced brusquely that the place had been sold. He told Lee and Bertha that he was going to live with his daughters in St. Paul. This crisis resembled an old-fashioned melodrama of the type that Lee's oldest son might someday publish. To Lee and Bertha, with three young children and no money of their own, it was a tragedy. (But three years later, he begged them to take him back into their home.)

Gathering up their few possessions, they moved to a rented house on nearby Edgerton Street and launched their own truck gardening business. Soon Larry was attending the small one-room school on Edgerton Street. Few people remember their first grade teachers, but LMB would never in his long life forget Miss Alice Ostergren. It was she who encouraged him to become a pint-sized orator, specializing in Eugene Field's "Seein' Things."

Obviously the blond, curly-haired youngster was loaded with talent. He was such a star at Edgerton School that Miss Ostergren began taking the little fellow to other schools to speak his piece. He would stand all by himself on the stage, and you could hear a pin drop as he widened his eyes and puckered his lips to match the spooky words:

Mother tells me "Happy Dreams!" and takes
 away the light,
An' leaves me lyin' all alone and seein' things
 at night.

At the age of five, most children are reluctant performers. How about little Larry Brings? Wasn't he afflicted with stage fright?

"Oh, no," said the immodest extrovert. "I wanted to get up there and show off! It felt good to see all those people listening to me—and hear the applause when I finished."

After about two years at the Edgerton Street address, Lee and Bertha Brings moved their growing family a few miles north to the area called Little Canada. What is the historical origin of that name—Little Canada? "Many of the early pioneers were French Canadians," Lawrence Brings will tell you. "Some of their descendants still live there."

In that placid rural community, before the advent of automobiles, Lee and Bertha settled down on ten acres to wrest a frugal living from the rich black soil and raise seven children who would become hard workers—with respect for God, financial independence and the better things of life that had been denied to their parents as a young couple.

The Little Canada property would become their permanent "home place." The purchase price was $2,500—a fairly large sum in those days. With careful planning, sixteen years later it had been paid in full. He remembers that his father always carried a roll of bills in his pocket even when he worked in the fields, because he didn't trust banks. As soon as his mother came home from the market, the vegetable money was promptly "deposited" in the pocket of her husband's overalls.

The bricklined house was quite snug. There were two bedrooms for the children—one for the boys and one for the girls. They had the ten acres of land, a few chickens, a cow, and two horses and a wagon. "One thing I never did," Lawrence recollects. "I never milked that cow!" That might eliminate him as a "man of achievement" right now.

Modern psychologists demand that youngsters be given "happy childhoods." Little Larry's mother didn't have time to read books about child psychology. She was too busy—raising vegetables as well as children. Perhaps she was born knowing that the best way to raise children is to keep them busy.

Besides, it was a struggle for survival in their case. "With all our hard work, my father's income was never more than $700 a year," Lawrence recalls.

What would Dr. Spock think of Lawrence's childhood memories? They are still vivid. "I remember all those vegetables—the rows of tomatoes, beans, onions, lettuce, and spinach. When I was ten or eleven years old, I was picking red, ripe tomatoes and loading them carefully into two bushel baskets on a wheelbarrow and pushing it two blocks to a shed."

The acres of vegetables must sometimes have seemed endless to Larry who, as the oldest child in the large family, had to be a "manly boy" so early in life. In addition to his own chores and duties, he directed the garden work of the younger children, weeding and cultivating rows of vegetables. The days of picking them did not lead to an evening of pleasant relaxation. Lawrence remembers helping his parents prepare the produce for market—cleaning and washing the shiny white onions, the green lettuce and spinach, the crimson tomatoes, and all the other vegetables they had picked that day.

There were strawberries, too, and several summers they had a field of raspberries. Some extra "hired hands"—about a dozen city youngsters—were needed to help harvest the raspberry crop. It was hard work, even drudgery by today's standards, but Lawrence Brings does not recall that it was dull. There was time for games and playtime activities. They made their own fun time.

The parents provided fun and humor for their children with games and music. Never to be forgotten is the time the father brought home a phonograph with two records which the children found fascinating and played them over and over again. Their father played the harmonica for family parties, and one night he brought home an accordion on which he played melodies without any previous musical training.

At Christmas time, the children made paper chains with flour paste and strung pop corn on string to decorate their Christmas tree.

For several years the highlight at Christmas was the arrival of Uncle Joe Harff, dressed as Santa Claus, bringing bags of toys for all the children. He drove a cutter and horse from the city to provide a happy Christmas for the poor relatives.

At Easter time they colored eggs with homemade dyes. During the winter months taffy candy pulls occurred frequently.

The day's work started early, when Lee Brings hitched the horse to the wagon and then went to work in the fields and to select the vegetables to be prepared for the next day's trip to market. Larry remembers his mother as the "driving force" in the family, in the truck garden, in the home — and especially at four in the morning when she would climb to the wagon seat and start for the farmer's market in St. Paul with an array of clean, glistening vegetables and fruit in the wagon-bed behind her.

"We had rented our own stall at the market," Lawrence said. "By the time everything was unloaded and arranged, the customers began arriving."

If some of the vegetables were not sold, Lawrence's mother knew where to find more customers. The resourceful lady would detour the wagon around the Italian neighborhood to sell tomatoes for making tomato sauce, and to the German neighborhood to sell cabbage for making sauerkraut.

After the sweltering heat of summer in the truck garden, young Larry always looked forward to the opening of school in the crisp days of autumn. From the age of five, the boy from the truck farm continued to enjoy the "feel" of words and the effect they would have on audiences. Being vocally articulate was not enough. He also took delight in the "look" of words. In his collection of boyhood souvenirs is a penmanship book, filled with carefully written exercises from his grade school days.

The important elementary subjects, during those "dear, dead days beyond recall," were reading, writing and arithmetic. The future would prove that Lawrence Brings received a well-balanced education and revealed a remarkable aptitude for arithmetic, especially when it came to stretching pennies into dollars.

His mother set an example for him. After the cow went dry in the fall, there was no butter for bread on the Brings' table. Ignoring the expensive prospect of buying butter, his ingenious mother would spread lard on the bread. Sometimes she would deepfry the bread dough. "It was especially delicious," her son recalls, "when she used sweetened homemade coffee bread and sprinkled a little sugar on it."

Another inheritance came to Lawrence from his mother's willingness to serve her neighbors in time of need. For years she was called on by mothers at childbirth to help care for the newborn baby and other children in the family. There were almost fifty occasions when she worked with Dr. Ostergren as a practical nurse during the births of children—and then stayed on in the home from a week to ten days —refusing to ever accept any compensation. No doubt the fact that her son during his lifetime has dedicated himself to give freely of his time and money when needs arose, can be attributed to his mother's example.

"Likewise, I recall," says Lawrence, "when a neighbor came to my father with a hard-luck story about losing his horse, whereupon my father offered to loan him one of his two horses, which would be a handicap to him in his farm work. The neighbor moved away and never returned the horse.

"We had no telephone and we prepared our school homework," says Lawrence, "under the dim light of kerosene lamps. But none of us suffered from poor eyesight. Our mother had purchased a family medical book from a traveling peddler and she used it to diagnose our childhood illnesses, and followed the remedies suggested. No doctor was called, except when a case of diphtheria broke out in the family."

The necessary periods of frugality did not cast shadows on Larry's childhood memories. The houseful of lively children and the turning of the seasons in the truck garden kept him on his toes. School was no problem, and he finished the eighth grade at the age of twelve.

Looking back through those years, Lawrence Brings recalls taking advantage of the "crests" that propelled him upward and onward—as though they were part of his destiny. Instead of shrinking behind his mother's skirts, he was an eager little orator at the age of five. After he finished the eighth grade at Rural School District No. 3 in Little Canada, what did the future hold for the bright-eyed, articulate youngster? There was another crest ahead.

If you had asked his relatives and neighbors, many of them would have said, "Now that Larry has had his schooling, he can spend all his time working in the truck garden. It's a good life's work for a strong, smart boy! What more could he want?"

Lawrence, himself, had been too young and too busy to think about his "life's work" yet. If he had any other hopes or ambitions, they remained dormant in his mind until the afternoon when his mother sent him on an errand to the teacher's house. The errand was trivial, but the consequences were something of a thunderbolt.

The years have not dimmed the memory of those moments in the teacher's kitchen. "I was ready to leave," Lawrence recalls. "I can still see Mrs. Loiselle standing at the ironing board, sliding the iron back and forth. Instead of merely saying good-bye, she paused and stared thoughtfully at me. Then she said, 'Lawrence, why don't you go to high school?' "

Almost speechless, the boy trudged along the dusty road toward home, thinking hard. Suddenly he wanted desperately to go to high school. He was elated about Mrs. Loiselle's confidence in him, and he was anxious to tell his parents—but what would they say?

He knew that his parents wanted the best possible lives for their children. He thought of his remarkable mother, who had been employed in the mansion of a St. Paul "lumber baron" before her

marriage. When relatives came to visit in Little
Canada, she would duplicate a Summit Avenue dinner party—from soup to fancy dessert. He thought
of the way his parents had encouraged all the children, making up in love and attention for the money
that was so scarce. His parents had worked so hard
to support a large family. In his mind was a picture
of his mother, dividing her busy days between housework, hoeing and cultivating in the fields, picking
and marketing the vegetables—and still finding time
to listen to the children and teach them to be better
workers and thinkers. Although Larry Brings did
not realize it at the time, his mother was an example
of self-propulsion that he would be inclined to emu-
late throughout his life.

Pondering the possible reaction of his parents,
with that dream of a high school education whirling
in his mind, the boy realized that life could swerve
in many directions—suddenly!

When he reached home and told his parents what
Mrs. Loiselle had said, they were as astonished as
their son had been. They had great respect for teachers. They were honored that their oldest son had
been singled out for such special attention. However, a truck gardener didn't need a lot of schooling.
None of the young boys in Little Canada had ever
gone to high school. If Larry went, he would be the
very first one!

At that time and place, in 1910, old Central High
School in St. Paul was a lofty crest—taking shape
in the distance—but a twelve-year-old farm lad
would rise to meet its challenge with a buoyant
spirit.

Starting school there in a suit of clothes his mother had made from a man's discarded suit, he discovered that he was dressed differently than his classmates, but he determined to overcome this disadvantage.

The slogan of McDonald's seems to characterize the potent force of thinking by Lawrence Brings, "Press on! Nothing in the world can take the place of persistence. Talent will not; nothing is more common than unsuccessful men with talent. Genius will not; unrewarded genius is almost a proverb. Education alone will not; the world is full of educated derelicts. *Persistence* and *determination* alone are omnipotent." These two words were to characterize his activities in the future.

Chapter Two

Daring to Dream

Lawrence Brings was born in an era when the young United States was beginning to flex its international muscles. With the nation stretching from "sea to shining sea," it even found itself in possession of a distant Pacific commonwealth—the Philippine Islands. It was an age of throbbing, aggressive growth. American railroads cut across deserts and through mountain passes, and American ships traded in foreign ports. Factories and farms were pouring out the fruits of American resourcefulness, and every boy dreamed of becoming an Horatio Alger hero—if he worked hard enough and had a little bit of luck.

The Brings children were born into that world, a different world—a world that seems incredible by today's standards. It was not so long ago in time, but the American Dream was still alive and thumping energetically in the heart of every redblooded American boy.

Nostalgia has become fashionable, but it cannot resurrect the true atmosphere of that age of innocence, discipline and ingenuity. Every bright boy looked for opportunities and took advantage of them.

Larry Brings did not loll around, waiting for services and favors. He had no time for boredom, no patience with futility. Nothing was futile if you cared about God, your country, and your ability to "amount to something."

To help them weather the storms of life, attendance at church and Sunday School were part of the normal pattern. To lead worthwhile lives on earth, to gain everlasting life in heaven—these were the highest ambitions of hardworking Americans. Lawrence's mother managed to get her three older children to begin Sunday School at Arlington Hills Lutheran Church which was then located on Payne Avenue. It was necessary for the children to walk four miles each way every Sunday morning. "A Mighty Fortress Is Our God," wrote Martin Luther. All the values seemed more substantial in the early half of the Twentieth Century, and somehow it was possible to be both idealistic and realistic at the same time.

Following his mother's example, young Lawrence Brings had already learned that "God helps those who help themselves." Just the effort of getting to Central High might demand super-human stamina. In a climate where the winters are harsh and daylight hours are short, Larry sometimes had to hike four miles each way, to and from the streetcar line—shielding his face from the blinding fury of a blizzard while he struggled through trackless snowdrifts.

Even in pleasant weather, it might be dark during the homeward trek. If Larry had been timid, he might have been "Seein' Things" all over again. He often recited poems and stories aloud, striving to develop his speaking ability and a firm, masculine voice. The high-pitched tones of his childhood refused to go away while his voice was changing—a situation that caused him intense anguish. He yearned to go out for debate and dramatics, but his shrill, weak voice was more comical than masterful. Nobody ever remembered that he had once been a star performer, but he was determined to regain his lost glory!

When the enterprising boy obtained a downtown newspaper route, delivering the *St. Paul Daily News*, his vocal frustrations did not keep him from being a good little businessman. He enlarged his route and hired other youngsters to lug the bulky bundles for him, and to deliver the papers to customers in special areas. His route included downtown business places, hotels, and even some "houses of ill fame" on old St. Peter Street. Sometimes all-night parties were still going strong in the hotels when he went around to deliver the paper Sunday mornings. "No matter who answered the door, I just thought of those people as *Daily News* subscribers," he says.

Larry's young life was a panorama of mixed blessings. During part of his high school years, relatives offered him a place to sleep in their St. Paul home so he wouldn't need to travel so far every day. In exchange for his unheated attic room, Larry took care of the furnace, shoveled snow, washed windows and worked as a handyman and kitchen helper. All this in addition to school and his newspaper route.

After he finally got to bed at night, Larry deserved to be told, "Little man, you've had a busy day!"

Larry had become active in the Sunday School at Arlington Hills Lutheran Church—so active that he was appointed Superintendent of the Sunday School while he was still a high school student. Because of Larry's duties there, the Rev. Nels Lundgren gave the young man a key to the church. It came in handy. Larry spent a few surreptitious nights in the church when it was difficult to walk home during a snow storm. After starting a fire in the furnace, he spread newspapers over the hot air register and slept on them.

When he was home during the autumn and the quickening of springtime, Larry was involved in the truck garden activity. Some of the vegetables had to be taken to market while school was still in session, and the young student could "hitch a ride" into the city with his mother at four in the morning. The glow of sunrise on trees and lakes, the horse and wagon, the boxes of dew-drenched vegetables and berries—these were healthy boyhood memories.

The boy's first experience in a high school expression class was a disaster. "My voice was so weak and expressionless that my speech teacher flunked me," he said. He still remembers her name—Miss Helen Austin—and he is grateful that she recognized the courage behind that poor little "changing" voice. He took the course again, with Miss Austin inspiring him to develop mature speech habits.

"I kept talking on my way home, sometimes shouting above the wind," Lawrence recalls. "I talked to the trees and the clouds—and delivered orations to the cows in the pastures. Whenever I was alone anywhere, I kept making speeches and reciting poetry."

Undoubtedly his voice would have changed in the normal course of time, but he was also gaining fluency and poise. His intensity of effort finally led to a pinnacle of glory. He was back on the stage again! During an interscholastic Shakespeare contest at the old St. Paul Auditorium, he brought "Bottom" vividly to life in a performance of *A Midsummer Night's Dream*. In subsequent comments in the school paper, it was noted that, "Lawrence Brings' voice carried to the back of the auditorium."

Instead of resting on those laurels, the young man kept practicing—projecting his voice, polishing his pronunciation, experimenting with tone and expression—whenever he had a few minutes of privacy. He had made a quick transition from truck gardener to scholar-orator. Clarity of thought became important. Lawrence set out to be a polished debater at Central High, and he succeeded because he taught himself to speak with logic and conviction.

Another of his triumphs was Hale's *Man Without a Country*. He not only dramatized the story for presentation as a play at Central High School, he also played the part of Philip Nolan, the storm-tossed hero of the story, at the school assembly. Undaunted by outside obstacles, Larry Brings made enthusiastic use of every minute of his school life.

Suddenly the young student was catapulted out of school and back to the house in Little Canada. When his mother became seriously ill for several weeks, Lawrence took the responsibility for much of the housekeeping—the cooking, washing, cleaning, and care of the younger children. The work in the truck garden had to continue. High school was something "extra," to be postponed in case of emergencies. Since it was difficult to get into the city every day, he had to give up his profitable newspaper route.

Under the circumstances, many a young person has dropped out of school forever. As soon as his mother had recovered her health, Lawrence returned to Central High, eager to catch the waning crest of the wave before it left him high and dry forever on the truck farm.

As he trod the halls of Central with appreciation, he wasted no time brooding because his former classmates had left him behind. He knew he had done the right thing at home, and now he was free to seek learning with renewed vigor. Only in the United States could a young person have such fine educational advantages, without money or family influence.

Shouting into the wind was no longer necessary. Larry could project his young male voice without strain to all corners of an auditorium, but he still practiced "talking to himself" in private. Dramatics, debate, and other public speaking activities were soon high on his list of extracurricular enthusiasms. Not since the age of five had he felt such surges of oratorical power within himself!

Lawrence's agility as a debater has already been immortalized in *Melvin J. Maas: Gallant Man of Action*, a biography about the former Minnesota

Congressman and Marine Corps General who was his classmate at Central. Lawrence Brings remembers the mock political convention of 1915 at Central High in which almost two thousand students participated during a day-long and evening program patterned after the procedures followed at regular political conventions.

He noted that it was more than just a one-day extravaganza. "For several weeks prior to the actual date of the convention there was exciting organization of the students into different political parties with the usual campaigning and maneuvering." Evidently the field was crowded with presidential hopefuls: "There were about seven groups who were campaigning for their candidates."

Larry Brings, Mel Maas and Donald Countryman were the three ringleaders who kept promoting a dark-horse party. Young Brings was chosen to nominate their candidate, Charles Evans Hughes, who actually did run against Woodrow Wilson the next year and later became Chief Justice of the United States Supreme Court—but not President. But the Brings speech won the nomination of Mr. Hughes. If the "fireball trio" of Brings-Maas-Countryman had been running his campaign, Mr. Hughes might have ended up in the White House.

In spite of the demands of school and the truck farm, Larry found time to be active in his church. He made good use of his God-given talents when he entered the Luther League speech contest as the representative of Arlington Hills Lutheran Church. In his essay entitled "The Treasures of Heaven," it almost sounded as though he wanted to take an oath of poverty:

". . . Oh, I beseech you, labor for your church that you may receive, as a reward, the treasures of Heaven. . . . Man will not be judged according to his gains and profits in the world but according to what he did and what he was in the world. . . . My dear Luther Leaguers, did you in the past, will you in the future, 'Lay up for yourselves treasures on earth' or 'Lay up for yourselves treasures in Heaven?' "

Larry's eloquent plea for celestial security made an impression on the judges and the audience, and he was awarded first prize. There were special compliments from Herman Samuelson, the distinguished Executive Secretary to Minnesota's Gov. Eberhart, who was one of the judges. Time would tell whether Larry's youthful idealism was an omen of his future character.

The proud possessor of a high school diploma in the spring of 1916, he stood again at the crossroads of his life—holding an unmarked map with roads leading mainly back to the truck farm in Little Canada. He was eighteen years old, and he had to take stock of his priorities.

As he worked among the vegetable patches that summer, the wheels kept going around in his head. He was not content. There had to be something more —a place for him, out there in the world. High school had whetted his appetite for a more satisfying, more mentally stimulating life.

His uncle Martin was manager of a downtown store, and whenever Lawrence dropped in to visit him after school, invariably he would say, "Lawrence, you're not going back to the farm after high school, are you? Don't you think you can do better for yourself?" Uncle Martin had been planting seeds of encouragement in the young man.

In later years, a Minneapolis publisher would sometimes describe impatient, restless people as "itchy." Back there on the truck farm in 1916, Larry had already become an authority on "itchiness."

One pleasant summer afternoon, he put aside his hoe and spoke to his father. "I want to go into town today," he announced. "I have an idea." He hurried down the long paths, changed his clothes, and walked the four miles that he knew so well, almost afraid that something might interfere before he reached the streetcar line. Would the truck farm always be a magnet—trying to lure him back, as though he had nowhere else to go?

Lawrence M. Brings was looking toward education as the foundation for his future endeavors. It seemed as though there should be opportunities out there in the wide world for a young man with an aptitude for assembling thoughts and delivering persuasive speeches. Did he dare to dream of anything like college?

The young man from Little Canada was taking his "idea" to the Arlington Hills Lutheran Church where he had been confirmed, served as Superintendent of the Sunday School, and felt very much at home. Would the pastor take him seriously?

Would he understand how desperately he wanted to go to college? Most of all, would he endorse his idea for earning the money he would need?

Evidently Lawrence delivered another convincing speech, because he received the encouragement he sought. The Rev. Nels Lundgren approved of his suggestion to solicit subscriptions for the respected "Lutheran Companion" published in Rock Island, Illinois.

"You may receive a forty percent commission on each one-dollar subscription," the Rev. Lundgren assured him. He was impressed with his young friend's ambitious attitude and wished him Godspeed.

Equipped with a list of potential customers in the Maryland-Arlington Hills area, the neophyte salesman went out that very afternoon and sold five subscriptions! Two dollars was a lordly profit for two hours' work, at a time when laborers were lucky to get twenty-five cents an hour. Selling magazine subscriptions has never been easy, but Lawrence's "gift of gab" must have shattered all barriers of sales resistance—especially among the members of the Arlington Hills congregation who knew him as their Sunday School superintendent.

Larger captive audiences were even better. By early fall, he was invading Ladies' Aid meetings with his persuasive little sales speech about the merits of the magazine as a moral influence and source of knowledge in Lutheran homes. He received "aid" from the pastors, too, because they were happy to introduce him and endorse his efforts.

Always, he was spurred on to greater successes by that "impossible dream" in his mind, that persistent obsession. He knew he had been fortunate to go to high school, but college was the new goal— the lofty crest—that crowned his vision of the future.

Lawrence did not have enough money to start school in September, so he went "on the road"—to Minneapolis, Cannon Falls, Stillwater and other nearby cities—living frugally, invited to stay in pastors' homes, stretching pennies, and hoarding dollars carefully.

The young salesman presented his credentials to the Lutheran pastors in each new community. He has warm memories of his first meeting with the Rev. C. E. Benson in Stillwater, Minnesota. After inviting him to stay for breakfast and listening with interest to Lawrence's reasons for being there, the the Rev. Benson said: "I'll walk around with you." With the pastor present, every parishioner subscribed. It was the beginning of a permanent friendship. The Rev. Benson was Chaplain at the State Penitentiary for many years and later a pastor in the Twin Cities. He is one of the people Lawrence Brings mentions with special affection.

Each new subscription brought Larry closer to the reality of college. Soon the magazine publishers, in faraway Illinois, took notice of their "star salesman" in the Twin Cities area. A cordial relationship was established, and Lawrence arranged to sell some of the books they published when he went out to solicit magazine subscriptions. It was another source of income.

By Christmas the energetic young salesman had earned enough money to buy himself a new suit of clothes and extras for twenty-five dollars. Self-interest might have been excusable, but he took pleasure in buying Christmas presents for his parents and all his brothers and sisters.

He had ninety dollars saved—to help his college dream come true. Because of his Lutheran Church connections, he decided to attend Gustavus Adolphus College in St. Peter, Minnesota.

There he was, a young man who was becoming accustomed to "crests" — to following his daring hunches to the sky-high limits of his imagination. It was unthinkable that the boy from Little Canada should be a college student. But there he was, at Gustavus Adolphus College on February 1, 1917.

Chapter Three

Earning a College Education

So Lawrence Martin Brings arrived at Gustavus in February, just at the beginning of the second semester. First of all, he hoped to convince the faculty that he could complete the first semester's courses as he went along. Believe it or not, he did, for he had already determined to earn his degree in three and one-half years. If anyone knew of his perseverance thus far, they would not bet against it!

By the time he had paid sixty dollars for the semester's tuition and purchased his textbooks, he had barely enough money left to begin eating and sleeping. There were no scholarships or government grants available. Larry managed to survive somehow by soliciting subscriptions in nearby communities and selling books for the Rock Island firm in his very spare time.

Although his parents were amazed and proud that he was so ambitious for a college education, he could expect no financial help from them. He does remember sending his laundry home in one of those brown canvas cartons—another bit of nostalgia. He ate for five dollars a week at a student boarding club and shared a room with a roommate at five dollars a month.

Was another crest looming ahead of him, unawares? Late in April, during his freshman year at Gustavus Adolphus, an upperclassman, Martin Larson, invited him to his room and "sold him" on the idea of becoming a salesman of Wearever Aluminum cooking utensils. He had never considered going into that kind of business, but it is obvious in retrospect that destiny was boosting him forward again. Young Brings was ready for it—he made a lightning decision to try selling pots and pans!

After paying the company a deposit of twenty-five dollars for two heavy kits of sample aluminum kitchenware, he was ready for business that summer.

Again, he was leaping ahead into unknown territory, heading south of the Twin Cities for Blooming Prairie where there were relatives who might help him as a last resort. If the young traveler had lost his way, he might have landed in a nearby town called Rochester, where Dr. Charles Mayo and his two sons were laying the foundations for a world-famous medical center.

Larry arrived in Blooming Prairie looking more self-confident than he felt. Fingering the last lonesome fifty cents in his pocket, he inquired about lodgings. Someone told him there was a widow, Mrs. Dock, who might have a room to rent, and she turned out to be a godsend. He still remembers how it felt: "When I carried my sample cases into the house, I was relieved to learn that she would 'trust' me for my room and board."

The widow had a lively personality, and she enjoyed helping Larry practice his culinary arts in her kitchen—including baking a cake on the top of her stove, and other surprising cooking stunts to demonstrate his utensils. Even though she had no "stake" in his success, she cooperated far beyond the call of duty.

"My landlady even arranged the first demonstration party in her own house," Larry recalls, "inviting housewives from the town. She knew everybody!"

Lawrence put on a splendid performance as a "chef." In addition to the company course of instructions, he had learned to cook for a large family during that period of his mother's illness. He confessed that he still feels dubious about one "demonstration trick" that was part of the act in those days: "I would jump up and down with all my might on a quart pan to prove that *all* my products were that indestructible. Actually it was a very fine line, and some of it that I sold in 1917 has survived and is still being used today."

With his conversational and cooking skills, the young man was a hit with the ladies. He made appointments to call on them and other potential customers in the area. To save wear-and-tear, he rented a horse and buggy for about 50 cents a day. "I didn't have to worry about 'gas' for the horse," he says with a twinkle. "When I drove into a farmyard, the folks would always give it feed and water."

The very first week, the amateur super-salesman made forty percent commission on $203 worth of kitchenware he sold. The last week of the summer, his sales leaped to a high total of $535. He returned to Gustavus Adolphus College in September as a bloated plutocrat.

Looking back, he remembers his quick decision to become a kitchenware salesman. Did his intuition tell him he would be successful? He still doesn't know. It would be a typical character trait all his life. "I took chances on the spur of the moment," he says. "I wasn't afraid to make mistakes." If it had been a mistake, it might have scuttled his hopes for a college education.

All along, there were crests of opportunity in his life that were significant, looming up to carry him farther away from the truck farm in Little Canada —with his impulsive cooperation. He had leaped at the opportunity to "speak his piece" before audiences at the age of five. The minute his teacher mentioned high school, the challenge became a reality in his mind. College was unthinkable for a penniless young man, but the reckless dream kept "cresting" until it took shape and form.

Lawrence Brings usually managed to be the right man in the right place at the right time. In addition to having a talent for salesmanship, it was a healthier age for door-to-door salesmen—an age of trust when people did not have to barricade themselves behind multi-locked doors and stare out at visitors through hidden peepholes. That dear departed age, when people seldom locked their doors, can only be remembered with wistful longing for its return.

The second summer, Larry was able to switch from the horse and buggy to the automotive age. He managed to latch onto a used Maxwell automobile; it wasn't too old because they had only started making them in 1912, and this was 1918.

During his Junior year at Gustavus, Larry was confident that he could afford to go to college by the fruits of his own enterprise. After two successful summers, the aluminum company honored their "champion salesman" with the offer of a district supervisorship. That meant he would sign up other salesmen, give them training lectures, and collect a five percent commission on their sales. Since everybody is not a "born salesman," he discovered to his dismay that his profits had been larger when he was doing his own selling.

Among the thirty-five salesman Larry signed up that summer was a young Hamline University student named Dan Gainey. After putting on a demonstration, Lawrence drove around with Dan in Dodge Center to give him a personal lesson in salesmanship and promptly sold three seventy-five-dollar sets of aluminumware during three calls one morning. "See, it's easy!" he told Dan. Now Lawrence adds ruefully, "But I was never able to duplicate *that* feat."

The years are marked with memories of the old days. Dan Gainey made enough money for college, and he met a special girl while he was working the Owatonna territory. After teaching physical education one year at Brainerd, Minnesota, he returned to Owatonna and married the young lady—a relative of the famous Josten family of Owatonna.

Lawrence's kitchenware travels had not led to any serious romances, but he fell in love with a picture! He was staying overnight with a friend, David Dahlin, in St. Paul at the time. Glancing around his friend's room, the visitor's eyes were drawn to a photograph of an attractive young lady in a place of honor on the dresser. Larry stared, pointed, and asked, "Who is she?"

"She's my girl friend—Ethel Mattson," Dave answered brusquely. It was obvious he wanted to say, "None of your business!"

Larry managed to glean two other grudging bits of information—that Ethel lived in Duluth and that her father was in the fuel business.

As though to assert his prior claims, Ethel's boy-friend settled down to write a letter to her. Larry could feel blasts of resentment aimed at him when he challenged Dave to do the same thing. "You don't even have her address," Dave fumed from across the table, "and anyway she wouldn't answer your letter if she got it!" Perhaps we should spare a tear of sympathy for that tormented fellow.

"I'll bet you a dollar she'll write to me," Lawrence challenged him. He addressed the letter to Miss Ethel Mattson, in care of the Mattson Fuel Company in Duluth.

In about two weeks, he received an answer from the young lady whose picture he had seen in his friend's room. When he went to collect the bet, it was the end of their friendship. Knowing about Larry's skill as a salesman, it's no wonder Ethel's erstwhile swain had been alarmed from the beginning.

The spark of romance began to glow, warmed by occasional letters, but there would be months of suspense before Lawrence could meet the young lady from Duluth who was as attractive as her picture—and musically talented besides.

In the meantime, Lawrence had a number of other irons in the fire—none of them having to do with romance. Debating and literary societies were popular on campuses at that time, competing with each other for social, oratorical and academic prominence. Research tells us that Lawrence Brings represented the *Clionian* Debating Society in an oratorical contest at Gustavus Adolphus on December 17, 1917. Among his opponents from the *Euphronians* were two young men named Luther and Benjamin Youngdahl who would also make their marks in the world—even though Lawrence Brings won that contest.

His proficiency as a public speaker brought young Brings an offer to teach at Gustavus Academy, a position he held for two of his undergraduate years.

During his sophomore year at Gustavus, he also walked straight into the publishing business. Deciding that the college should have some attention in the local papers, he went to the editor of the weekly *St. Peter Free Press*. As a result, he became campus reporter for a section called "News on the Hill" during his college years.

Larry didn't get paid for writing, but he got all the newspaper space he wanted. The publisher had two sons who took care of the shop—one was the typesetter and the other the pressman. It was a small, informal business, and the young student was able to practice setting type and operating the presses. Notice the way he took advantage of his opportunities to acquire valuable skills, even when he didn't need them. He approached everything with imagination and curiosity.

After awhile the resourceful young student started soliciting advertising in an effort to "localize" his income, and he got paid for that. When the editor of the *Free Press* went away for a week, Larry was asked to make up the front page. The editor was so pleased with the result that he thought his young reporter should go into the newspaper business. "Why don't you buy me out and become the publisher of the *St. Peter Free Press?*" he suggested.

Larry looked at him in astonishment. "Buy you out? I haven't any money. And aren't your sons interested in carrying on the paper?"

"They like the technical side of the business best. And don't worry about money right away. You can pay me as you go along. And I'll stay on as editor."

Lawrence M. Brings was still wondering what his life's career would be, but publishing a weekly newspaper did not give him a very "cresty" feeling at that time.

He kept searching the field for a future profession that would appeal to him. "I had an idea that I might want to study law," he said. "I liked to talk— to make words work for me." That would mean more years of study, but it would have suited his talents.

The most skillful use of words, both in speaking and writing, became the "LMB trademark" in college. In addition to his experiences as campus editor with the *St. Peter Free Press,* he was business manager of the senior annual—successfully selling $4,000 in advertising. The result was that each of his classmates received a refund of the ten dollars advance they had made to underwrite the project. There was enough profit remaining for a gift of $500 to be given to the college.

As an ROTC officer at Gustavus, he had charge of the military drill of his company and the administrative work that went with it. He held a Captaincy in the Reserve Officers Training Corps and served for a short time in the Army before the end of World War I.

A multitude of his activities leaned toward public speaking and various stage and platform endeavors. He was president of the Inter-Collegiate Prohibition Association and won the State Prohibition Speaking Contest at Macalester—a victory that qualified him for the national finals in Nebraska.

Young Mr. Brings placed second in the State Oratorical Contest with an oration entitled "The Triumph of the Common Man" in which he proclaimed:

> The course of human achievement may be defined, and the experience of countless ages may be interpreted by the declaration that from generation to generation freedom has been the one grand aim of "all man's struggles, toils and sufferings." Liberty has ever been the watchword of advancing civilization as it makes its way with increasing momentum up the Rugged Mountain of Progress.

He believed that a "common man" could triumph, especially if he spelled his "crests" with capital letters. And capitalized on them!

Lawrence was elected treasurer of the College Missionary Society, and President of the *Clionian* Debating Society—naturally. He was manager of the Lyric Male Chorus Concerts at St. Peter, and President of the American College Students Loyalty League. (Where have all *those* students gone?)

It boggles the mind to contemplate the total extent of Larry's extracurricular activities, especially when we remember that he was trying to get his degree in three and one-half years, supporting himself and paying all his college expenses, and even managing to save a portion of his earnings as a kitchenware salesman. Pots and pans might seem mundane to housewives, but they were something else to Larry Brings. "That position," he says, "gave me valuable training in salesmanship, human relations and management." Gustavus Adolphus gave him scholarship status. But, long before he was graduated from college, he taught himself to be "a man of experience" in the business world.

Lawrence enjoyed going home to Little Canada to see his parents and bask in the family atmosphere whenever possible. It was a special place, he remembers. "We always had a feeling that our parents cared a lot about us. They taught us to be a close-knit family unit, working and sharing together, and not neglecting each other." The younger sisters and brothers were growing up, and there were always new developments to discuss.

Larry never ceased to be amazed at his mother's boundless energy and imagination. In her own way, she was more daring than he! On one of his trips home from college, he was startled to see that she had bobbed her hair—before it became a popular style everywhere. Some members of the family were shocked about it, but Bertha Brings said it was a nuisance to take care of long hair. So she turned out to be the Irene Castle of Little Canada!

Chapter Four

A Romance for All Seasons

Lawrence Brings finally met his lady fair from Duluth when she came to Minneapolis to continue her musical education. Already a gifted concert violinist, Ethel Mattson had soloed with the Duluth Symphony Orchestra. Larry had learned that Ethel was not the only musician in the family. Her talented sister often accompanied her on the piano.

The Mattson family sounded almost too glamorous and sophisticated for a boy from a Little Canada truck farm. If he had ever suffered from stage fright, this was the moment for it—but he had come far and had developed boundless reserves of self-confidence.

Even before their first date, Larry and Ethel discovered they shared a fascination for "play-acting" in their personal lives. Their first "script" featured drama, humor and intrigue.

Ethel had already arrived in Minneapolis, and some mutual friends—the Bergquists—knew that Larry was anxious to meet her. They invited the Gustavus student to their St. Paul home for Sunday dinner, promising him that Ethel would be there.

Larry already had Ethel's new address. In a mischievous mood, he wrote to her and suggested that they get together on the night *before* the dinner. He added, "Wouldn't it be fun, when we get to the Bergquists, to act as though we've never seen each other before?"

Ethel knew there was nothing dull about this young man. A fun-loving girl who appreciated jokes, she quickly agreed to the fiendish plot.

Larry came up from St. Peter to Minneapolis on that fateful evening and got a room at the "Y." Then he met Miss Ethel Mattson and escorted her gallantly to a performance of "Maytime" at the Metropolitan Theatre. Perfect entertainment for a rapturous first date with a musical young lady.

"We had a wonderful time," Lawrence recalled pensively, "and then I took her home on the streetcar." Even in this modern age, a note of nostalgia lingers.

Their eyes shining with secret glee, the conspirators gave an outstanding performance when they were "introduced" to each other at the Bergquist home the next day. Their hosts beamed, completely convinced that they had brought the two young "strangers" together at last!

After Ethel returned to Duluth, they didn't see each other for almost a year. Spring, summer, winter, fall—the seasons turned so quickly—but frequent letters wove bonds of affection across the miles.

During his last college year, Larry was seeing Ethel more often. When he went to Duluth, he was invited to her home to meet her family. It was a hopeful sign, but she was so talented and so popular.

Lawrence's heart was filled with pride when Ethel visited her cousin at Gustavus Adolphus and played the violin at convocation. He was delighted with the ovation she received, and certainly he applauded loudest of all.

The romance became a matter of utmost importance to young Brings. That recollection is still clear in his mind: "When it looked as though Ethel might consider marrying me during her visit to St. Peter, I lured her into the entryway of my rooming house on some pretext or other—so we could be alone for a few minutes—and proposed then and there," he confided.

He was prepared in case she would say yes. On an impulse, he had spent all his money on a diamond engagement ring! He wasn't going to take a chance that she might change her mind. For a young man who had always been careful about money, this had to be love! It was impulsive, as usual, but it was good planning.

Lawrence and Ethel were a devoted young couple, even during their engagement. They wrote to each other every day, and they kept their collection of letters as family souvenirs for many years.

Marriage would have to wait until Lawrence had made a decision about his future career. He still thought he might study law, but he was getting some tempting job offers.

He had received a letter from the head of a large national shoe company. The man had heard about his activities and offered him a respectable salary to start, with assurances of rapid promotion. That was not exactly what he wanted.

The Aluminum Company of America invited him to be their representative in the Scandinavian countries, selling hotel pots and pans, but he talked it over with Ethel and she didn't want to live in Europe. "Besides, I couldn't speak any of the Scandinavian languages," said Lawrence.

Lawrence's promotional talents were recognized by the Minnesota city of Willmar. He was asked to consider a position as public relations manager by Victor Lawson, the local newspaper publisher, promoting good feeling between Willmar and the surrounding rural community.

In the spring of his senior year Larry was still eating at a boardinghouse with nine or ten of his friends, most of whom were accepting teaching positions. The more he listened to their animated discussions about their high school jobs at $100 to $110 a month the more exasperated Larry became. It was evident that other members of his family had been bitten by the "education bug" when he demanded, "Why do you want to accept such low salaries? My little sister, at 18, is getting $115 a month for teaching in a one-room country school, with a one-year Normal School teaching certificate."

They continued talking about all the advantages in the teaching profession and sounding superior about their own qualifications. After listening until he was getting bored, the iconoclast in their midst pushed aside his plate that day and bet he could get a higher-paid teaching job than any of them—even though he had taken no education courses. They grinned. He must be joking.

He took out a dollar bill. "We'll each contribute a dollar. Mrs. Schwarz can hold the stakes. When I come up with the highest salary in the group, I'll win the whole ten dollars."

They laughed and told him, "Kiss your dollar good-bye!"

When young Mr. Brings made a decision, he allowed no grass to grow under his feet. He immediately began evaluating his qualifications. What could he contribute to the teaching profession? He could teach speech, and he had become familiar with a wide variety of subjects—including psychology—at Gustavus. As a salesman, he could "sell" students on the idea of wanting to learn, to accept challenges, to make the best use of their abilities.

Lawrence Brings realized that his connection with the *St. Peter Free Press* could be used to advantage. He wouldn't have to spend tedious hours at the typewriter, making dozens of copies of his biographical resumé. Instead, he composed a concise description of his curricular and extracurricular achievements, including his ROTC and Army service record, and listed all the offices he had held and the awards he had won during his college career. He also emphasized that he was an experienced, successful salesman.

In parentheses, he inserted pointed little remarks such as, "Executive ability developed—can handle men and train them," and, "Can take charge of military drill and training if desired" in case the school had an ROTC program.

Because he had bothered to learn "unnecessary skills," he was able to set his scholastic Achievement Record in type and run it off on a job press in spare moments between writing "News on the Hill" and selling advertising for the St. Peter weekly. The resumé was neat and easy to read, and the recipients must have thought, "This is a very resourceful college student!"

He also enclosed copies of letters of recommendation that he collected from various members of the faculty, the principal of Gustavus Academy where he taught speech to the young people, and businessmen who were familiar with his exuberance for work.

How did young Mr. Brings look, on the eve of graduation? What were his social and moral habits? We know from his pictures that he had curly brown hair and good features. The other information was packed into a terse paragraph entitled *Personal data:* "Age, 22; Birth date, Sept. 29, 1897; Weight, 160 pounds; Height, 5 ft. 7 inches; Health, good; single; American; do not dance, play cards or use any form of tobacco." Evidently he got all his "kicks" from talking and debating.

In addition to sending applications to likely-sounding schools, Larry signed up with two teachers' agencies. In every instance, he emphasized that he would not accept less than two hundred dollars a month—a fantastic amount in 1920. At that time, it was tantamount to declaring that he didn't actually want a teaching job!

Certainly he was "playing hard to get," and it brought results. Suddenly he was notified that he had been elected the superintendent of schools in Hope, North Dakota, at a salary of two hundred dollars a month! How could he bluff his way through that kind of a position? "I turned it down," he says, without regret.

The teaching offer that appealed most to him came from New Richmond, Wisconsin. He was informed that they could not exactly pay him two hundred dollars a month, but he would receive its equivalent, a salary of $190 a month—plus a bonus of $90 at the end of the school term. It added up to the minimum he had specified.

The day the contract arrived, Larry took it along to the boardinghouse. Seated at the table, he signed his name with a flourish. "There it is!" he told his astounded friends, inviting them to inspect the document. After it had been passed around the table and scrutinized with care, they had to admit he had won his foolhardy bet. Grinning smugly, he collected his money.

He says, now, that he was "operating on brass" when he accepted the New Richmond position. He still had other options that might have been viewed as more prestigious.

Toward the end of his senior year, the President of Gustavus Adolphus College summoned young Brings to his office and stunned him with the announcement that he had a natural talent for the ministry. "You are the type of man we need in the church!" Dr. O. J. Johnson declared. Lawrence had been active in religious groups on the campus and he had spoken in churches—in addition to everything else—during his college years.

The church had always been an inspiration to him, but he had not considered it as a future career. For once, he almost stuttered when he told the college president, "But I haven't felt a call to the ministry!"

Figuring that Lawrence had been numbed by that theological thunderbolt, Dr. Johnson told him to think about it and come back the next week for another discussion.

How would it feel to be addressed as "the Rev. Brings" for the rest of his life? "I faced the fact that it would be satisfying to my ego as a speaker," LMB recalls, "but I didn't feel that God was leading me in that direction."

He admitted that he hadn't exactly felt a "call" to the educational field either—that it was a case of "sheer guts" when he launched that fantastic job-hunting campaign and landed the New Richmond contract.

Commencement time at Gustavus in 1920 was a super-miracle for one persevering young student from Little Canada. There he was, sparkling with the joy of achievement, his name inscribed on a genuine college diploma. *Lawrence Martin Brings, Bachelor of Arts!*

He would not celebrate his twenty-third birthday until after the start of the school year at New Richmond, the following September. Considering the time he had missed during his mother's illness and the half-year of selling subscriptions to finance his entry into Gustavus, he had reached this peak of scholarship with as much speed as his classmates. In addition, he had developed a variety of valuable skills above and beyond the college catalog—everything from successful salesmanship to writing news stories and setting them in type.

Chapter Five

A Glorious Year—1921

The young Gustavus Adolphus graduate settled down to teach social sciences and public speaking in New Richmond, Wisconsin, a town in the beautiful St. Croix River valley, not far from the Minnesota border and the Twin Cities. It was much farther to Duluth where Larry's fiancee lived, but an amazing development enabled him to see Ethel every weekend.

The Lutheran ministry kept reaching out to Lawrence Martin Brings, even though he hadn't gone to a divinity school. Dr. Johnson had arranged for him to fill the pulpit every Sunday at Trinity Church in Duluth. He would be paid one hundred dollars a month, plus railroad fare. It was miraculous —he enjoyed "preaching," he would be well paid, and he would be right in Ethel's home town! Perhaps this was a loud, clear call to the ministry.

He did not neglect his teaching duties at New Richmond. The challenge to be a better teacher was boiling in his blood. He enjoyed working with young people and sharing his enthusiasm with them. Most of all, he encouraged them to speak up, to be articulate. After "monitoring" some of his classes, the superintendent at New Richmond marveled at the way all the young people were stimulated to take part in class discussions.

"I had to keep ahead of those high-spirited kids!" Lawrence recalls. By treating them as though they were extroverts with worthwhile ideas, he increased their self-confidence as individuals.

His teaching philosophy gained fame in that area, and two school superintendents came to sit in the back row of his classroom to observe his techniques. After building a reputation as "a remarkable instructor" during that first year of teaching, he started receiving offers from high schools at Eau Claire, Wauwatosa and Milwaukee, Wisconsin.

Professor Brings was a champion orator himself, and he insisted that his speech students be equally confident and persuasive when they stood up to speak. Instead of trying to dominate them, he urged them to share his beliefs in the magic of words.

As a result, the brand-new teacher—who had taken no education courses in college—coached a debate team that jolted the "big-name" opposition for the first time in history. The headlines, at the top of the front page of the *New Richmond News*, jubilantly proclaimed:

NEW RICHMOND HIGH SCHOOL WINS
CHAMPIONSHIP OF THE NORTHERN HALF
OF WISCONSIN IN DEBATE BY 14 POINTS

According to the story, "The situation was full of thrills" right down to the finish line. "The long distance telephone wires were sizzling hot" as New Richmond held its collective breath in suspense. When the final opponent, Rice Lake, was eliminated it meant that "New Richmond is getting into the big games and must trot with fast company from now on to win the state championship."

And who was responsible for that remarkable performance? The news story ended with a tribute to Professor Brings who had charge of debating in the New Richmond High School. "Our winning teams are demonstrating the excellence of his coaching," the reporter declared.

Lawrence Brings also coached a star orator, Norman Beebe, who reached the Wisconsin State Championship finals in Madison.

As for the course that used to be known as civics, the young teacher brought his social studies class to life with community involvement that was far ahead of its time. He was a "modern practical ecologist," urging his students to participate in anti-pollution campaigns—checking the alleys of New Richmond for ashes that needed dumping and garbage cans without lids. His students headed a clean-up drive, gathering facts and figures and reporting sanitation abuses to the Town Council. Professor Brings made them realize they should take pride in the beautification of their home city by preserving and enhancing their scenic heritage.

In the meantime, there were those exciting weekends in Duluth. Larry would usually board the train north to Duluth on Friday afternoon and spend part of Saturday and Sunday at Ethel's home. The two days in the Lake Superior city became crowded with church activities when he was also asked to instruct the confirmation class on Saturday afternoons because there was no regular pastor.

On Sunday morning, the visiting minister could look down from the pulpit and see Ethel sitting in the congregation. Actually, they were managing to keep their engagement a secret. As far as his closest friends knew, Lawrence Brings went up to Duluth to fulfill his pastoral duties—and that was it!

After church on Sundays, it was the custom for the members of the congregation to invite their young pastor to dinner. Some of them were leading citizens in Duluth, and he remembers them as "very fine, intelligent people." When they urged him to continue for another year, it was difficult to tell them he felt more at home in other areas of activity.

Toward the end of his first school year at New Richmond, the life of the teacher-pastor began rising toward a new summit. His good friend, the superintendent, advised him to get out of New Richmond! He was not being fired or rejected. "You are just too rich for our blood," he was told. "You should be teaching in college, where you would have wider scope for your talents. With your advanced methods, you could be making a worthwhile contribution to higher education."

It sounded pretty illogical to Lawrence, but the superintendent offered to help the young speech teacher find a college faculty position.

Larry Brings went through the same routine again, joining teachers' employment agencies, gathering recommendations and character references, compiling a new resumé. This time he didn't specify a

minimum salary, because he wasn't betting that he'd
get a college instructorship!

During that year at New Richmond, he had been
quietly toying with the idea of going into business.
It had started with a tempting offer from the Capital
Service Company, an Investment Securities firm in
Boston. The Vice President, E. G. Leffler, wrote:
"We are casting about for a man to handle our house
organ, clients' journal and Daily Bulletin." Lawrence Brings had been recommended to him. According to Mr. Leffler, the former editor had "worked
up to a $5,000 position, and has now been promoted
to a position in our ranks which should be worth not
less than $25,000 a year." Those were giddy figures.
Mr. Brings would have to start at a modest salary,
but they expected him to be a "repeater."

LMB seriously considered staking his future
with Capital Service; he sent inquiries to Commonwealth Trust and State Street Trust in Boston to
check out their financial reputation. Judging from
an old souvenir copy of the Capital Service Company
Bulletin which dealt with "enthusiasm," Lawrence
would have been the right man for that job. He could
agree wholeheartedly that a man should "trot out
his enthusiasm and give it a thorough course of
calisthenics in order that it might be in good trim
for the day's activities."

The correspondence with Boston tapered off.
Lawrence was too busy in New Richmond and
Duluth that year. After his conference with the New
Richmond superintendent, he barely had time to
gather testimonials to accompany his application for

a college teaching position. As it turned out, he had more staunch boosters than he had ever dreamed!

Dr. E. C. Carlton, Head of the English Department at Gustavus Adolphus College, wrote: "Mr. Brings is a man of sterling integrity and honor. He possesses to a very high degree the qualities of enthusiasm, initiative and enterprise. He is a scholar of very high attainment and of splendid intellectual endowment. In manner he is cordial, sympathetic, and cultured. He is approachable and possesses plenty of tact. In appearance he is prepossessing. His business ability is highly developed and I have never known him to fail in an enterprise or undertaking which he has entered. I commend him most highly to anyone interested."

Dr. S. L. Reed, who had been Larry's psychology instructor at Gustavus, mentioned traits that are still apparent: "I regard Mr. Brings as a young man of exceptional native ability and attainment. Perhaps his greatest asset is his boundless energy. He is a hustler—always occupied with something. At school he had the capacity and the ambition to do about three men's work—as an orator, a debater, officer in the Reserve Officers Training Corps, business manager of the senior annual, promoter of religious activities, as a student, etc.—all in one year. In addition to this he assisted in teaching in the Academy for two years. It is of course needless to say that some of his regular work as a student suffered but when all these activities are taken into consideration he did remarkably well." And Dr. Reed forgot to mention Larry's time-consuming connections with the *St. Peter Free Press!*

Back in 1921, psychology instructors showed respect for religion and morals. Dr. Reed continued with a new burst of exuberance: "Mr. Brings . . . is morally sound and has a very positive attitude towards morality and religion.

"His chief interests are along the lines of English and public speaking. He is by far the best that Gustavus Adolphus has produced in recent years. He is a pleasing and fluent speaker with ideas and force. He has a very pleasing voice—both as to volume and quality."

Bertha J. Schei, the Principal of Gustavus Academy, was a lady of charming brevity: "Lawrence M. Brings gave entire satisfaction during his two years of teaching Expression in Gustavus Adolphus Academy, 1918-1920. Besides the regular classroom work, he coached the speakers in declamatory contests. He took an active part and interest in his work and possessed the ability of inspiring the students to greater efforts and higher ideals."

Dr. Heber S. Mahood, Pastor of the Congregational Church in New Richmond, reached lofty heights with these rhetorical praises: ". . . Mr. Brings is one of the finest and cleanest cut young men I have met in recent years. Any institution that possesses a man of this type is a fortunate school indeed . . .

"Mr. Brings is a young man with a winning personality, a fascinating smile, a strong spiritual nature, a force, a determination and an adaptability that carry him through seemingly impossible places. What he starts out to do he has created a reputation of doing.

"One of the finest religious addresses I have been privileged to hear for a long time was delivered by Mr. Brings in my church just a few weeks ago. His addresses in other churches have been equally inspirational and effective. In this way his influence in and out of the schools has been most remarkable.

"I assure you we find no ray of delight in Mr. Brings' proposed change, but we know he is equipped for larger work, and we also know the institution which is fortunate enough to secure his services will have no regrets to offer."

Much to Lawrence Brings' surprise, a number of colleges were impressed with his credentials and the enthusiastic letters of recommendation — even though he was only a year away from Gustavus. On the same day he was offered a position to head the Speech Department at a salary of $2,500 a year at South Dakota State, and at Northern State Teachers College at Aberdeen, South Dakota, where the salary was only $1,000 a year, but he would have complete freedom to give private speech lessons and keep 90% of the fees. Whether it was impulse or intuition, he seemed aware of his capabilities and the environment in which he could reach the highest levels of accomplishment, and he was confident of his ability to accept a challenge.

Soon the Aberdeen contract was safely signed and sealed. The news was announced, and the New Richmond paper saluted the departing teacher with this farewell message: "Professor Brings has made a splendid impression during his year in New Richmond, has done excellent work here, and he will be much missed."

New jobs may come and go, but marriage is a lifetime business. A continuing romance reached its grand climax on August 26, 1921, when Ethel Mattson and Lawrence Brings were united in holy matrimony in a formal ceremony in Duluth. Many of their relatives and friends joined in the wedding celebration, beaming their approval and wishing them happiness. Larry's former classmate, Hugo A. Carlson, later reminisced about the event:

> How well I remember the day! That romance was a secretive one as far as we at college were concerned. We knew he was a frequent visitor to Duluth, but the object of his affections was camouflaged by his Sunday ministry there . . .

Hugo also mentioned that Larry tried to get him interested in one of the bridesmaids at the wedding. Even then, Lawrence was noted for his "promotional ability." His successful courtship resulted in a broken heart for at least one of Ethel's suitors. That particular man vowed, "If I can't marry Ethel, I will never marry anyone." They didn't think he meant it.

Chapter Six

A Giant Step Forward

When the newlyweds arrived at the railroad depot in Aberdeen, South Dakota, they were surprised and delighted to receive "celebrity treatment." President and Mrs. H. W. Foght were there to welcome them to Northern State Teachers College, a four-year accredited college with approximately 1600 students and 100 faculty members.

Professor and Mrs. Brings rented two rooms in a boardinghouse as their first home. "Ethel didn't have to bother about housework," Lawrence recalls. Later, she assisted him with private speech lessons and gave violin lessons.

The professor prepared immediately to take charge of speech classes, debates and plays. With his urge to do things that were bigger than life, he plunged into the academic schedule with enthusiasm.

During the first month, he was disappointed that none of the students seemed interested in private lessons which he had hoped would give him a more adequate salary. Perhaps they were waiting to see whether he had something special to offer—a magic formula, perhaps, for transforming ordinary talkers into dynamic spellbinders. His classroom technique soon proved that Professor Brings believed *anyone* could learn to express his opinions with authority and self-confidence.

We asked, how did he do it? Could he give me an extemporaneous sample, here and now? That request brought forth a dazzling display of facial and vocal fireworks. The former speech teacher was not afraid of words; he dominated them, wringing the ultimate in fury, humor, and tenderness from each important syllable. His impromptu demonstration proved that nobody should handle words timidly; they were meant to be gripped by the lips and tongue —and unleashed with intensity. Words and phrases were fascinating tools. If they were manipulated properly, they would flame, crackle and roar.

For instance, most people would read a phrase like "the wail of the wind" in a normal monotone. Not so with Professor Brings! He would twist his lips and wrestle those w's with his tongue. Listening, you could hear the e-eerie w-w-wail of the w-w-wind; in your "inward eye" you could see the trees tossing their branches to the rhythm of the words. Try the same techniques with "'the r-r-roar of the l-l-lion." Poetic phrases aside, a machinist could talk eloquently about "w-wheels going 'r-r-round and 'r-r-round."

Professor Brings would lecture his students: "How are words created? Out of human experience, of course! Words are the re-creation of physical and mental existence. How would you transform words into reality? You must *see* what you are saying! If you want to speak with authority, you must learn to re-create reality—with all its drama and shades of meaning."

Where did Larry Brings develop such a masterful relationship with the English language? Who taught him? "Some of my teachers encouraged me, but I actually trained myself," he says. It went back to those very young years when he recited "Seein' Things"—with the kind of lingering, spooky emphasis that made juvenile and adult audiences eager to listen to him again and again.

It was a revelation to hear that he originated all those complicated speech skills that were so advanced, so imaginative. There were reminders of the times he had talked to the wind and the cows on the way home from school: "I taught myself to savor words and phrases, and concentrate on their qualities. As I said before, I practiced whenever I had a chance, from the time I was a youngster in the first grade."

Almost everyone has had experience with speech teachers in high school or college, but it is doubtful that they had the same tenacious grip on the subject that Lawrence M. Brings had. Usually they just ordered their shuddering, shivering students to stand up and speak to the class. They didn't try to arouse flaming sparks of inspiration, of compulsion—of almost feverish dedication to the fine art of public speaking. They didn't keep saying, "You must re-create reality, or you won't get your message across —no matter how significant it is!"

The students at Northern Normal, as well as local citizens, began to realize that Professor Brings could add a priceless dimension to their business and social lives. He soon was swamped with private lessons, starting at 5:00 a.m., for students and local business and professional people. Bashful students might hesitate to contort mouths and torture their faces in class, but the one-teacher, one-student ratio provided an ego-bracing atmosphere. Professor Brings insisted on elocutionary exaggeration during speech lessons—making certain that enough of the extravagant emphasis would be retained to make normal communication more animated and persuasive. His definition was: "Public speaking is merely uninterrupted enlarged conversation."

On November 18, 1921, Professor Brings took time off to speak at the Armistice Day exercises in Webster, South Dakota. Rather than merely sending him ten dollars for his expenses, E. A. Wearne of Webster added this tribute: "In extending to you the hearty thanks of the community, I but voice the general expression in saying that your address was a masterly production in both thought and construction and its delivery was an oratorical treat such as we seldom enjoy in a town of this size. Your visit will certainly not detract from the popularity of the Northern Normal School."

Larry Brings was glad to speak at patriotic observances, even though he sometimes wasn't paid at all. Judging from the rousing phrases in this Memorial Day address, he cared more about inspiration than remuneration:

> Comrades and Friends: This is the fifty-seventh annual Memorial Day. The American people will show once again their love for and their gratitude to the men and women who died

in the nation's service as defenders of the country. It speaks with marching men, with dirge and anthem, with flags aglow, with tears and cheers, with flowers for love, with surge of grief and resurge of pride, with words of gratefulness for what has been, and with pledges for what there yet should be . . . American soldiers who sleep in hero graves died for peace, not for war; for honor, not for lust for power; for principle, not for dominion; for democracy, not for autocracy; for justice, not for material gain . . ."

The new faculty member worked long, hard days, arising in the winter darkness to meet with students who wanted private speech lessons, but it paid off in money as well as in the satisfaction of knowing he was helping students to be better equipped for the challenges of life. By the end of the first year, Professor Brings was earning a larger income than the president of the college!

As a dramatics coach, he often worked late at night, turning awkward young people into confident Macbeths and Hamlets who had learned to "re-create the reality" of Shakespearean drama.

He developed an aggressive debating team that was eager to "do battle" with all comers. When Professor Brings heard that a team of championship debaters from Redlands University in California would be touring the Midwest, he asked Dr. Foght for permission to invite them to Aberdeen. "Oh, no," the college president said. "They can't be defeated!"

Coach Brings took that message back to his debaters, and of course they refused to accept it as final. They met the champs and emerged victorious.

Macalester College was considered another formidable foe, but they won that encounter and others.

Lawrence and Ethel taught during the summer
sessions as well as the regular school year. The Summer School Bulletin, in 1922, listed Lawrence M.
Brings as Head of the Department of Speech and
Director of Forensics and Dramatics, and Ethel I.
Brings as "Associate and Instructor in Private Lessons in Expression."

The Department of Speech offered a Public
Speaking Course which was "Intended to develop
a pleasing voice, good enunciation and the ability to
express thoughts before an audience." Professor
Brings' students would learn that the bland decrip-
tion in the bulletin was a whopping understatement.

Another popular course for teachers dealt with
all phases of Thespian activity—principles of selecting plays, making up, costuming, and direction of
plays. The class performed one-act plays for the
summer school students.

The individual lessons in Expression and Dramatic Reading were not "snap courses." In addition
to payment of a special fee, a student needed a "B"
average in other classwork to qualify for two hours'
credit.

A half-century later, that 1922 Summer Bulletin
from The Northern Normal School must be a col-
lector's item. There are pictures of male professors
in high, stiff collars. The faculty ladies wore fashionable shirtwaists, in an age when their skirts swept
the campus sidewalks. Typing and shorthand were
featured in the Bulletin, but dictaphone machines
had not yet been invented. Greek and Hebrew His-

tory were respected subjects—as well as American History, of which there was much less in 1922.

Educators had their troubles in those days, too, but there is an optimistic, idealistic tone to the "Introductory Note" in the bulletin: ". . . In recent years the United States has gone through a great transition during which teaching has lost some of its high social and professional rank. Indifferent protective legislation, increasing amateurism and resulting low salaries are largely the cause. The war has changed all this. America has come to see that education is the true cornerstone of democracy and that the professional teacher is the nation's real benefactor."

An overflowing school schedule did not diminish Larry Brings' old zest for extracurricular activities. Because he had served for a time during World War I and was interested in other young veterans, he became an active member of the American Legion post in Aberdeen.

A popular speaker everywhere, the professor sometimes "doubled" as minister at one of the Lutheran churches in Aberdeen and devoted time to religious programs and projects.

One of Lawrence Brings' finest achievements was the organization of the South Dakota Speech Association. His devotion to the speech arts brought him into contact with leading educators in other South Dakota schools. One of them was a young professor named Karl Mundt who was a member of the faculty of Eastern Normal in Madison. Lawrence recalls visiting at the home of the future United States Senator and enjoying lively conversations with his articulate colleague.

At the beginning of his second year at Aberdeen, the local representative of Metropolitan Life persuaded Lawrence to test his speaking skills on insurance prospects—in his spare time. Since he could talk so well, he should be able to sell Metropolitan Life policies without too much difficulty. Almost immediately, Lawrence sold a $1,000 policy. When he dropped into an Aberdeen bank, the president asked him how he was getting along. By the time they had finished talking, the neophyte insurance salesman had sold a $10,000 policy to the bank president! It was a neat trick, because the bank had its *own* insurance department.

That type of successful salesmanship attracted the attention of the "high brass" at Metropolitan Life. One of the supervisors made two trips to Aberdeen from Minneapolis to try to persuade the speech teacher to accept a position as manager of its Duluth office. Lawrence suspected they had done some detective work and learned it was his wife's home town. "How many men are operating out of your Duluth office?" he asked.

"Four or five," he was told.

"And you want me to supervise them? They would resent me—a younger man with no experience. Aren't some of them better qualified for the management job?"

The other man replied, "None of them has your intelligence and enthusiasm!"

He always had that extra ingredient—enthusiasm. Making a profit was important, but he wanted to enjoy himself on the way to the bank. He threw himself, heart and brain, into every project he tackled, trying to learn all the angles and intricacies of that particular subject. Dullness, he has always believed, is a bad habit that should be avoided by staying mentally stimulated, seeking new goals and challenges, and moving forward with discipline and good-humored aggressiveness. He has never been *blindly* enthusiastic. As a publisher in later years, he could read "off-beat" manuscripts with appreciation, but he was always aware of the ultimate question: "Will it sell? Will it be appropriate for our market?"

Larry Brings decided he was not passionately excited about managing an insurance office, and he turned down another opportunity to move to Duluth when Ethel told him, "Dad would like to have you go into the family fuel business." He undoubtedly would have been a great success at that enterprise —if he had felt inclined to be an enthusiastic fuel dealer, which he didn't.

He was a man who wanted to guide, to enlighten, to inform. At that time in his life, he cared most about the teacher's role as an instrument for building character and encouraging young people to aim toward greater goals. Every student and teacher possessed a tongue and mouth, and he felt they should strain themselves to make the most of that special equipment.

At the end of the summer session in 1923, Lawrence bought a used Ford for $100, and he and Ethel headed back on those well-remembered gravel roads toward the Twin Cities. The car was a Model T "convertible" — with attachable isinglass window panels. In s-s-stormy w-w-weather, the w-w-wind w-w-wailed through the cracks!

It was supposed to be a vacation trip, but Lawrence has never learned the difference between business and pleasure. Previously he had been interested in the Minneapolis School of Music—mainly as a bystander and as a student of Mr. Holt in speech classes. In 1923, Mr. Holt, one of the two owners of the school, was fatally injured on a mountain climbing expedition, so Lawrence bought his half-interest in the institution and became its president and head of the dramatic art department.

In addition to visiting the School of Music during that trip, Lawrence had promised to do a favor for a Dakota Wesleyan friend, Mr. Veatch, who had applied for a position in the Speech Department at the University of Minnesota. Knowing what a convincing talker Lawrence was, the other man had asked him to deliver a personal recommendation to Professor Rarig, the head of the Speech Department.

Lawrence Brings, with his usual enthusiasm and sincerity, overdid the job. Just as he opened the door to leave, fate hoisted him "crestward" again. "Wait a moment," Professor Rarig said. "Why don't *you* apply for that position in our speech department?"

Although Professor Rarig wasn't standing at an ironing board, it was a "reenactment" of that scene in the teacher's kitchen in Little Canada — when Larry was twelve years old. As he started to leave, she had asked the boy, "Lawrence, why don't you go to high school?" If he hadn't heeded her advice, he wouldn't be standing in the Speech Department of this prestigious university listening to another earth-shaking suggestion.

As he had done on similar occasions, Lawrence now looked at Professor Rarig in amazement. "But what about the man I've been recommending?" (It was almost a case of, "Why don't you speak for yourself, Brings?")

Professor Rarig waved his hand airily. "I'll send him an explanation, but where can we get in touch with *you?* What is your telephone number here?"

In a couple of days, the phone rang and a now-familiar voice said, "Rarig calling. You have been elected to a position in our Speech Department at the University." Just like that!

Coming from a much smaller school, Lawrence knew it was a terrific honor to be chosen for a faculty position at the University of Minnesota with its huge student enrollment and burgeoning campus high above the Mississippi. Almost overnight, he found himself poised on the giddy heights of a new crest.

With an active interest in the Minneapolis School of Music, as well as a speech job at the University of Minnesota, Lawrence tried to think of a diplomatic way to leave Northern Normal. He had already signed a contract with the college, and he attempted to cancel it gracefully by sending a telegram while he and Ethel were on their way up to Duluth. It turned out to be an awkward situation. Dr. Foght replied that he expected him to return and refused to take "No" for an answer.

In an eloquent letter, Professor Brings pointed out that the University position was a professional advancement. He would also need to be available at the Minneapolis School of Music—now that he was half-owner and would be teaching speech classes there.

Lawrence and Ethel felt saddened when they went back to Aberdeen to pack their belongings and say good-bye to the handful of friends who were still speaking to them. Northern State Teachers College had been an important promotion in 1921, and they would always be grateful for the memory of those two lively, rewarding years.

Chapter Seven

Teacher of Speech, Professional Lecturer and Entertainer

Still a young man in his middle twenties, Lawrence Brings found himself on a crest that demanded mature poise and fortitude. His term of "probation" at the University of Minnesota required that faculty superiors monitor his classes periodically. When the new speech teacher checked with Dr. Thomas, the head of the English Department—with which the Speech Department was affiliated—he learned that practically all the reactions were highly favorable. There was one grumpy critic who said he gave each student too much individual attention—which was exactly what LMB kept striving to do! It was the secret of his success!

During his five years on the faculty at the University, his influence reached out in all directions—to churches and centers of learning all over the countryside. He laid the foundation for a happy speech-teaching relationship with Northwestern Theological Seminary that would last for twenty-seven years, and at Luther Theological Seminary for twenty-five years.

How many hundreds of ministers would credit Professor Brings with much of their future eloquence in the pulpit? It wouldn't be proper to lay them end to end, but future endorsements would prove they would stretch far—and go far in the ministry.

Did any of those future pastors ever suffer from stage fright? Let us look ahead several decades and see that bread cast upon waters may return with a thick layer of icing on it. At a Rotary meeting in 1971 the president introduced Lawrence Brings to a guest who exclaimed, "Your name is a household word in our family!"

"I hope it's not a bad word," Lawrence responded.

"We always speak of you with deep gratitude," Bruce A. Peterson assured him. "You probably remember my brother Joe, from South St. Paul, who attended your evening classes many years ago. He said you gave him the kind of self-assurance he needed. Your prize achievement was our younger brother who was too bashful to open his mouth in public. You gave him so much self-confidence that he decided to go to college. He was graduated from Gustavus Adolphus College and is now a successful minister!"

The Brings philosophy was beneficial for everyone, in a variety of everyday circumstances. For several years, he conducted evening speech classes for the members of the Minneapolis Dental Society and the American Institute of Banking. At one point, he was giving speech courses to management people at the Dayton Company. He put them through exercises to relax their muscles, emphasizing that muscle tension was all tied up with poor personal control.

In the business world, he also noted, it was a good idea to disarm and control antagonism with a soothing voice. "This," Larry Brings said with a twinkle, "is especially true in the case of women— who are more emotional."

As a successful salesman himself, he takes a dim view of high-pressure fellows who try to bully customers with aggressive "sales pitches." He has his own technique for halting the haranguers: "I always interrupt them in a calm, low-pressure tone of voice, and it stops them cold. After that, it is possible to talk on a conversational level." Communication, he believes, is a matter of compensation—of maintaining a civilized verbal balance on the scales of human relationships. That approach might be applied with wisdom to modern international diplomacy.

As a young faculty member at the University of Minnesota, Lawrence Brings had never considered becoming tremendously active on the lecture circuit. "That again was accidental," he recalls.

He was attending a faculty reception when circumstances nudged him toward another new crest. Dr. Lotus D. Coffman, the President of the University, was asked by Dr. Brown, a former classmate at Indiana University, who was Coffman's guest, to recommend a convocation speaker for an appearance at St. Cloud Teachers College.

At first Dr. Coffman seemed stumped as he looked around the room, and then his eyes lighted on the new member of the Speech Department. He must have been impressed by Lawrence Brings' enthusiasm as a speaker, because he said, "We have a new man on the faculty who might be perfect for that

St. Cloud speaking date. Go ahead, see if he is available."

Lawrence confided that he was prepared to talk about a pet subject—"using the teacher's voice as an asset in teaching"—any time, anywhere. LMB had noticed that teachers are more likely to concentrate on *what* they are saying, rather than on *how* they are saying it. Without the proper emphasis, lively information could sound bleak and dull.

Professor Brings enjoyed reaching out to students and sharing the benefits of his explorations into the adventurous world of rhetoric. After he had spoken in the morning to the students, he appeared before the St. Cloud Kiwanis Club at noon with a program of impersonations. He was asked to accept an invitation for a return engagement for the next summer session.

When he returned to the college to pick up his check before starting home, he was gratified by the complimentary remarks of the man who had invited him to St. Cloud. "Young man, you have something!" he was told. "I am going to a meeting of Normal School presidents next week, and I'm going to tell them about you." The result? He was invited to speak at each of the five state Normal Schools.

A highlight of the activities at Moorhead State Teachers College during the summer session of 1924 was the appearance of Lawrence M. Brings. On July 7, he addressed the convocation on "Oral Interpretations of Literature." In the evening he read "Macbeth" from the auditorium stage.

During that summer, young Professor Brings found himself in constant demand as a lecturer at leading teachers' colleges and universities in Minnesota, Wisconsin, North Dakota, South Dakota, Montana, Colorado and Wyoming. What was the great attraction?

"Audience involvement" was often a highlight of his talks. On the spur of the moment, he would ask an English teacher to choose five or six books of poetry at random and bring them to the lectern. Even when he opened the volumes to pages that were strange to him, he demonstrated that unfamiliar verses could be read aloud, with dramatic comprehension, by training the brain to think in terms of width and depth of eye span while accentuating key words and phrases. This, of course, was a first brave leap toward the age of "speed reading." In addition to the emphasis of an educational philosophy, it was providing entertainment for his audience and invariably won audience applause because of the novelty of the performance.

In his appearances before teachers and normal school audiences, Professor Brings was ready and willing to discuss a long list of enlightening pedagogical subjects, including: "Speech Disorders in Children and How to Remedy Them," "Blending Oral and Silent Reading," "The Teacher in the Community," "Building a Live Vocabulary," "Can a Teacher Keep Young?"

After the first crowded summer as an educational lecturer—with some dramatic readings and civic club dates thrown in—Lawrence Brings found it difficult to hop off the lecture circuit when school started. Audiences seemed eager to hear him, but the days were not long enough and the pace was getting hectic. In desperation, he went straight to the President of the University of Minnesota for advice. He said in effect, "Look what you started!"

Dr. Coffman, who recalled that he had recommended Lawrence for that first appearance at St. Cloud, was delighted to receive rave reports from other institutions about his success. "Go out as much as you can," Dr. Coffman told the popular young speaker. "Other people can take your classes when you aren't here. We need men of your caliber to represent the University."

That was equivalent to being told he could go out for recess any time—to do what he enjoyed most and get paid extra for it. His starting salary at the University was $2,500 a year, but the lecture engagements would soon bring it to exceed the $6,000 he had earned during the second year at Aberdeen.

As an "authority in the speech arts," Professor Brings sometimes discussed "How to Coach Plays." It was a topic that was dear to his heart because he cared about staging first-rate entertainment—as a director, or as an actor who could impersonate all the characters in the play.

His one-man interpretations of dramatic classics could have been a full-time career. The Brings repertoire of plays, as listed in a lecture bureau brochure, included: "Journey's End" by R. C. Sherriff, "The Fool" by Channing Pollock, "Street Scene" by Elmer Rice, Shakespeare's "Macbeth," and Shaw's "Candida" and "Androcles and the Lion." And later there were several more plays added to his repertoire.

In his solo readings of all those roles, did Professor Brings go racing around the stage? Did he stand first in one spot, and then turn and "talk back to himself?" No, he did it the hard way. He stood facing the audience all the way through, which is an art in itself. "I portrayed each part by changing my facial expressions and using different degrees of inflection, tone and resonance," he recalls. The voices of his women characters were modulated, without the exaggerated falsetto that some impersonators consider necessary. He managed, with talent and sensitivity, to "play" all the voices as though they were instruments in a symphony orchestra.

The mood was sustained, bringing accolades through the years from a variety of discriminating audiences. In describing Professor Brings' interpretation of "The Fool," Dr. J. A. O. Stub of Central Lutheran Church in Minneapolis wrote: ". . . In certain sections of the dialogue the people scarcely breathed. It was one of the most powerful, at the same time heart-searching hours many of us has spent. Prof. Brings possesses a splendid vocal organ, and he knows how to use it in an inimitable manner. His diction, enunciation and expression almost instantly make you feel that here is a master in the use of that Divine gift, the human voice."

In a moment of sober reflection we remember that Dr. Stub and many of the people who applauded Lawrence Brings have taken their own last bows on the stage of life, but the eloquence of the written words can still be cherished.

After his performances, young Mr. Brings often received "rave notices" in the local newspapers. According to the *Estherville Enterprise* of Estherville, Iowa, "Mr. Brings captured his audience with the reading of the three-act play, 'Candida.' . . . One man voiced the sentiments of everyone when he said: 'Mr. Brings made each character live through his vivid interpretation.' "

The *Times-Record* of Valley City, North Dakota, referred to him as "a master in the art of reading and interpretation."

He made a hit in Kansas, too. The *Ellis County News* reported that he "apparently adapts himself as easily to one characterization as another with the result that he entertained his audience thrillingly . . ."

The audience in Pella, Iowa considered him a man of at least two dozen faces—all in one evening. After he appeared at Central College in Pella, the paper reported: ". . . He presented the play in such a manner that we could easily distinguish all twenty-five characters with no effort on our part . . . To hear such an interpreter is not only educative but an inspiration."

The Lamoni Chronicle of Lamoni, Iowa, analyzed the Brings technique in its review: "Lawrence M. Brings brought to his audience a real message in the dramatic interpretation of 'Candida.' He relies entirely on the voice and facial expression to convey thought and feeling. With one so skilled in the use of the voice, the interest of the audience was easily held from the opening until the end of the three-act play . . ."

Mankato, Minnesota, loved him, too. The *Free Press* said in superlatives: ". . . It was a marvelous performance and the rapt attention of his listeners testified to his remarkable ability to hold an audience."

The resourcefulness of the self-trained dramatist was described by the St. Olaf College *Manitou Messenger* of Northfield, Minnesota: "With only a small platform for a stage and only miscellaneous gymnasium apparatus for a scenic background, the lone actor was able to grip and carry his audience with him to such an extent that they forgot that they were confined within the bare and drab walls of the St. Olaf college gymnasium."

Flora H. Krueger of the College of Education at the University of Wyoming wrote him a fan letter: "May I say that your interpretation was the finest thing I have ever heard! Your power of presentation was such that I visualized that play as clearly as if I were witnessing a stage performance. You are a master in your work."

Acclaim from other educators revealed that he was broadening the horizons of scholarship for his audiences. Of Professor Brings' "highly effective presentations of dramatic literature" during several summer sessions at the University of Minnesota, Professor Irving W. Jones wrote: "We find a growing interest in good drama; we wish to present more of it, if not in stage performances, at least in a spoken form. Our students respond heartily to it, indicating that they, too, want it. But especially do they appreciate such work as your own which has been among the high spots in our summer program."

President J. N. Brown of Concordia College at Moorhead, Minnesota, considered Professor Brings "a distinct inspiration to us, not only by your reading of Friday evening, but also by the conferences you held with our students and members of our faculty. We need a stimulus of that kind once in awhile to cause us to think along new lines and undertake new problems."

Dr. F. J. Kelly, Dean of Administration at the University of Minnesota, had this high praise for Professor Brings' presentation of "The Fool": "The predominant quality was its evident sincerity, the genuineness of the interpretation, and the absence of all superficiality. A piece of literature handled as you handle it is sure to mean to the audience almost 100% of what the author had in mind . . ."

The secretary of the YMCA in Minneapolis considered Lawrence Brings' programs the highest form of entertainment. He wrote: "I feel that if we are able to announce several of your interpretive readings as a part of this winter's series, it will add a great deal to the success of the whole course."

As he went rushing from platform to platform and lectern to lectern, there is no record that he was ever short of breath or boundless enthusiasm. His pictures show him, at that time, as a bright-eyed, dignified young man.

When he reached the same age, the Brings' son and heir, Keith, would appear to be a "second edition" of his father. Lawrence missed that great moment in every father's life, the birth of his child, in 1925. He was on a two weeks' lecture tour in the East and received the news during an appearance at Kent State University in Ohio.

His sister-in-law phoned him that everything was under control. "Ethel says, finish your tour!" Ethel was as capable as she was talented. When it came to handling a crisis, she didn't play "second fiddle" to anyone.

Since he was always booked in advance, the show had to go on—in large cities and small towns, in auditoriums and gymnasiums. After "researching" all the glowing testimonials he received, a biographer might conclude that education lost a great speech therapist, and the stage lost a great actor, when Lawrence Brings gradually turned his energies toward business and administrative interests.

According to *Who's Who in America,* Professor Brings received his Master's Degree from Gustavus Adolphus College in 1925. How was that achievement possible, when he was juggling a full load of lecture dates, speech classes at four Twin Cities colleges, and church and civic activities? "I was given a series of special assignments by Dr. E. C. Carlton, the head of the English department. I made my reports to him by correspondence and personal conferences," he says casually. "Then I managed to put a thesis together, 'The Origin of Place Names in Minnesota.' " How to get a graduate degree on the run!

The brief reference to "church activities" is misleading, because Lawrence's devotion to the development of Central Lutheran Church in Minneapolis would almost place him in the same category with the cornerstone. Only four years before Lawrence and Ethel became members, a dozen founders had begun to hold services in a rented church, working with spiritual zest and zeal to build a congregation. Their minister was the brilliant, eminent Rev. J. A. O. Stub who had answered their humble call after World War I.

Pastor Stub was still the spiritual leader, and the congregation was considerably larger when Professor and Mrs. Brings first attended services at "Old" Central Lutheran in 1923. In later years, Oliver Prestholdt told how it had come to pass: "Several of us were members of a public speaking class led by Mr. Brings, and we discovered that he was a Lutheran. We needed a Sunday School superintendent, so we invited him to meet with our teachers and we convinced him to accept. He and his wife later joined the church on October 17, 1923." Those words have much greater meaning in the years to come.

He held the position of Sunday School superintendent for several years, but it was only the beginning of his involvement with the "legendary" downtown citadel of worship.

Chapter Eight

He Founded His Own College

Lawrence Brings did not find his association with the Minneapolis School of Music as rewarding as he had hoped it would be. In 1926 he asked his partner to buy him out.

Spurred onward by an urge to develop a specialized speech school, he decided to establish his own. No sooner said than done. He founded the Northwestern College of Speech Arts in Minneapolis, incorporated as a nonprofit institution. The name was more impressive than the original equipment. "We set up business with a card table and a couple of folding chairs after renting several classrooms at 68 South 11th Street in Minneapolis," Lawrence said with a smile, still amused at his youthful audacity. The president and director of the new college was less than thirty years old.

One faculty member and about twenty-five students deserted the School of Music speech department and followed Lawrence to his new speech college. As enrollment increased and expansion was necessary, the Northwestern College of Speech Arts purchased the property at 2600 Portland—the former Savage home of twenty-six rooms.

Even the hardships are happily remembered. "Those were good years—great years—when we were struggling to make a success of our speech college," LMB recalls with enthusiasm. "We worked hard, but we could see progress. We got some instructors from the University to join our faculty and built up a four-year accredited course, certified by the Minnesota Department of Education. The dramatic and speech department in the Music School had been only a two-year course."

The new school emphasized the Brings speech-teaching philosophy. "Our students studied the basic principles of speech and developed them into a fine art," Lawrence said. He spoke of Marianne Pries, a young student at that time who became a lifelong colleague and friend in the Brings enterprises. His voice "re-created" the memories, bringing beloved scenes to life in "vocal" color: "Marianne and all those students were talented! They learned Shakespeare in the old traditional style and rhyme—they looked and sounded as though they would be at home in the Elizabethan Age." A member of his student body was John Qualey who became a well-known motion picture character actor, and many others became professional actors in New York and London.

Marianne Pries was a talented thespian in her own right and revealed skills as a speech instructor and play director while she was still a student. Larry and Ethel asked her to stay on, as a faculty member and administrative assistant. She proved so indispensable that she is now an executive officer in the present company.

Back in 1928 and during the precarious years ahead, little Keith Brings had an unusual upbringing. Instead of hiring a baby-sitter, Ethel "took him to college" with her. "Keith used to play under the table in the office while we were working," Marianne remembers.

Those were years of intense effort and industry, with undertones of nervous exhaustion and over-tones of gallant merriment. All work and no play might have turned the low-budget enterprise into a disaster, but the dauntless threesome kept a sense of humor. The members of the struggling young company proved by their attitudes that the burdens of hard work could be lightened by a whimsical ap-proach to their daily chores.

Lawrence Brings was not the only "good talker." Ethel and Marianne flew through their labors with lively bursts of conversation, sometimes punctuated by gales of laughter. "We kept running into funny things in the office," Marianne explained.

She remembers with amusement that their girl-ish laughter once aroused complaints from several students who were trying to study in the adjoining classroom. They informed Professor Brings that "the office help" was too noisy and spent too much time having fun while he—"the big boss"—was away on lecture tours. "They didn't know that Ethel was his co-partner in the firm," said Marianne, still laugh-ing about that episode.

Lawrence continued to go out on the lecture cir-cuit to supplement the Speech College income. He was actually keeping the college afloat with his lecturing funds.

His powers of concentration must have been incredible, because he continued to give polished performances—instead of worrying about "the wolf at the door" of his speech college.

LMB's play-reading tours to high schools and colleges demanded much stamina, but he considered them profitable. He often gave two readings at schools in the morning, two in the afternoon, and performed at a PTA meeting in the evening. He charged twenty-five dollars for each appearance— and kept putting the money back into the college treasury.

He was always a popular speaker at two-day teachers' county institutes in Iowa where he would be one of two "headline speakers." He considered himself well paid, because he received $250 for each two-day session, reading a play, meeting with English classes, and dispensing speech-training advice to teachers. Afterward, he would head his Model T back toward Minneapolis and the hectic schedule at the College of Speech, Northwestern Seminary, Luther Theological Seminary, and a variety of random speaking dates and extracurricular activities.

Marianne remembers that her "boss" gobbled up stacks of work with furious energy. After evening classes or play practice, some of the faculty and students went out for coffee about eleven o'clock. If they happened to return to the school after midnight—or even at one in the morning—they usually would see the President of the Northwestern College of Speech Arts seated in his office, pounding away at the typewriter for dear life.

He trained himself too well; to this day he cannot bear to dictate letters or use a dictating machine. Unless he pours the words directly from his brain onto the typing paper, he is not satisfied with the results. He says he saves time by *not* dictating letters, reading them, editing them, and then asking a secretary to type them all over again!

To keep expenses down, all the permanent staff members at the speech school were expected to be multi-talented—and Larry Brings didn't give them a chance to sit around getting rusty. He had already established a pattern of working long days and far into the night, and it was contagious. When they weren't coaching plays and teaching speech classes, most of the faculty members worked in the office.

Everybody around Lawrence Brings kept branching out into new territory, as he did, when he organized play casts for the Newton Company, and directed several professional play companies for Chautauqua. Marianne remembers their tight schedules when some of them went on the Chautauqua Trail in the late 1920s. Since radio was in its infancy and there was no television competition, the arrival of the huge Chautauqua tent in any small midwestern town was the great event of the summer. The performers and other acts were "booked" by national entertainment agencies and were scheduled for appearances on certain days during Chautauqua Week. The towns were asked to guarantee a five-hundred-dollar "gate." Anything over that amount was divided among the performers.

Chautauqua was considered "family entertainment"—rated "G." There were comedies and tearjerkers, magicians and gospel preachers, trained dog acts and musical programs.

Comedies were popular, and Marianne's troupe scored a hit for a whole season with "Pigs." She recalls that several cast members had to "double" in minor roles, when there weren't enough actors to handle all the parts. Signe Shaler, who is still with the Brings firm, was among that gallant company—cruising from town to town and from state to state, in a big Chautauqua van. Sometimes the next appearance might be a hundred miles away, but the show had to go on.

"No matter how sick we felt," Marianne says proudly, "we never missed a performance." Once, when their van broke down, they had to hire a horse and buggy—but they got there!

Up through North Dakota, out to Wyoming and Montana, back through Nebraska and Iowa they went, and on to Wisconsin. They usually presented matinee and evening plays. If they were in a town on Sunday afternoon, they were asked to sing hymns for an hour and a half. Luckily four of them had "barbershop harmony," and they were the kind of actors who knew plenty of hymns.

With Lawrence Brings training them, they had learned to be versatile and flexible. Sometimes they were asked, on the spur of the moment, to lengthen their programs for an extra hour. They would go into a huddle and come up with a quick skit to fill the gap.

"Larry Brings took pride in our dramatic performances," Marianne recalls. "Whenever possible, he would meet us on tour and check on our performances. He didn't want us to get in a rut, always interpreting plays in the same old way."

It was a challenge to keep trying to surpass themselves, as well as the competition, on the Chautauqua circuit. Local officials and audiences were polled on their favorite acts, and the agencies kept close track of the results. "We always rated high," Marianne said. "We were considered disciplined performers who would always keep our dates and put on a good show. One summer we kept going full-blast, from May 20 to Labor Day, and we were rated top favorites, to the credit of the superb direction of Lawrence Brings. Our reward was a chance to perform for two days at the State Fair."

Her eyes sparkled as she told about overflow audiences that stretched far beyond the uplifted tent flaps—as far as the eye could see. That was an age when Chautauqua had its own "spectaculars," never to be forgotten.

As radio gained a foothold, the Northwestern Drama Group got into broadcasting, presenting a play on a Twin Cities station every Sunday afternoon. Never in history was speechcraft more important in "re-creating" scenery and emotion—in sharpening the imaginations of the listening public.

Lawrence Brings says he was operating on "sheer guts" when he founded the College of Speech Arts, with no wealthy contributors or educational grants to help with the financing, but with a board of local citizens as trustees. His school achieved recognition and even some national prestige as "the only institution of college rank in the West to devote its entire attention to the teaching of speech arts."

According to a college mailing piece which listed "Ten Reasons Why You Should Attend Northwestern," the curriculum aimed to develop the personality of each student and promote leadership qualities. Classes were limited in size, and each student received the personal interest and attention of every instructor.

It was franchised by the Packard Theatrical Institute of New York City, which would assure its graduates of a reputable "Broadway contact" it they wished to pursue a professional stage career.

With full accreditation from the Minnesota State Department of Education, Northwestern graduates were qualified to teach speech in high schools.

The students had their own newspaper, "The Northwestern Spotlight," and the school had been honored by the installation of Zeta chapter of Phi Mu Gamma, National Honorary Dramatic Sorority.

Northwestern held classes twelve months a year, daytime and evening. It conferred two-year Associate diplomas, as well as degrees of Bachelor of Arts in Speech Education and Bachelor of Oratory upon completion of the four-year courses. The fifteen "artist teachers" on the faculty were recognized as "great platform artists, lecturers, actors and pedagogues."

From all the "historical evidence," Lawrence Brings always put on a "good shew" when he stood up in front of a public speaking class. In answer to an inquiry from a Council Bluffs, Iowa, businessman who asked for information about the speech courses,

John A. Miller of McGill Lithograph Company wrote that he had been a member of one of Professor Brings' evening classes for two and one-half years: "During this time I have seen many earnest men come and go from his classes and without exception, they have been very enthusiastic about the results . . . Mr. Brings has many students that are outstanding in the life of Minneapolis, and their advancement has been quickened by the instruction of Mr. Brings."

Mr. Miller's personal experience was cause for gratification. "I consider my work under Mr. Brings and the accomplishment gained therefrom invaluable, as I was making progress under very serious handicaps . . ."

Writing on handsome bond paper, Laurence F. Stanford, a Minneapolis insurance man, told Lawrence Brings how much he enjoyed his "painless instruction" in Practical Speaking. "The weekly classes were as entertaining as they were valuable," he wrote. ". . . The actual practice has helped me greatly in overcoming timidity—sometimes bordering on panic—which I used to feel when called upon to deliver a few well-chosen words." Mr. Stanford was looking forward to resuming the classwork in the fall.

Earning money for his college had to be important, but we get the feeling that LMB enjoyed his work tremendously. He was rejuvenating the lives of "shrinking violets" who usually sat in the back row at meetings—so nobody would ask their opinions. A poignant example is the letter from T. J. Godfrey of Hibbing, Minnesota, who acquired a new personality after he heard LMB address the Hibbing Kiwanis Club. "It might interest you to know that the writer had never addressed this or any other club, but after hearing your talk, I managed to hold the floor for twenty minutes at the next meeting," Mr. Godfrey wrote. "I informed the members that I was able to do so, after hearing your instructions . . . And since then I have talked to four other luncheon clubs . . ." Professor Brings was paid ten dollars, plus expenses, for making that trip to Hibbing.

Another "miracle of articulation" was wrought in the life of L. A. Wilkie of Continental Machine Specialties in Minneapolis. Mr. Wilkie sent good news about "a letter I'd like to frame"—in appreciation of his own talk on mass production at a business meeting. It might have been considered a dull subject, but Lawrence Brings' coaching hints had taught Mr. Wilkie how to hold the rapt attention of the audience by accentuating the human interest angles.

Mr. Wilkie's tribute to LMB should also be framed: "Now, I believe credit should go where credit is due and your training course is entirely responsible for my ability as a speaker. Three months ago I would not have been able to say 'Jack Robinson' before our club or any group of more than four persons. I would have been petrified (mentally and physically, except in the knees) in the attempt. You have proved conclusively . . . that you can make a real speaker out of most anyone . . .

"The weekly classes are always interesting and entertaining and I would rather attend one of them than a good show. This is to notify you that I have appointed myself to a committee for the purpose of heralding your course to everyone."

After the President of the Northwestern College of Speech Arts spoke at a Sigma Nu Phi dental fraternity meeting at the University of Minnesota, the members decided to descend on the school in a group for a series of speech lessons. Their reasons were made clear in the following announcement:

"Those of you who know Mr. Brings are aware of the fact that he has exceptional ability along this line and that he is able not only to *tell* you how it should be done, but his many years' experience as a public speaker enables him to *show* you how, which is very important . . . I think we were all in accord in changing 'Our Secret Ambition' to be able to speak and act as he does. If atmosphere and environment mean anything, it is a foregone conclusion that those of us who spend ten or fifteen hours with Mr. Brings will have acquired an asset that will be invaluable to us in the future."

There was a "very nominal charge" of one dollar an hour for each man, in classes of ten or fifteen Sigma Nu Phi members. It should be remembered that it took longer to earn a dollar from thirty to fifty years ago, when the Great Depression was casting its shadow over the country in the form of unemployment and dust storms, but Lawrence Brings undoubtedly gave much more in speech benefits than he was paid. From the information in the following episode, he may have helped countless men to weather the Depression through increased self-respect and word-power:

In the middle of February 1931, the Minneapolis speech man held classes for two days at a convention of Giant Manufacturing sales representatives in Council Bluffs, Iowa. According to an enthusiastic letter from one of the Giant directors named C. J. Farr, he sent all 150 salesmen back to their national territories "prepared to surpass all sales records of the past."

Mr. Farr continued to laud the speech instructor: "You can feel justly proud of what you have done . . . Our men have received the finest course in speaking that could possibly have been given them . . . Each and every one is singing your praises. We believe the standing ovation you received at the close of your final talk was justly merited.

"You took 150 men and in two days' time gave them a practical course in speaking that will mean many dollars to the organization. You took several fellows shivering with fright on the platform, and in two days you had developed confidence and poise. Personally, I don't believe we can place a dollar value on what you have done for us . . . We have profited very much from the two days that you were with us, and we will recommend you to any organization training salesmen . . ."

Lawrence Brings, master of dynamic rhetoric, was conducting a one-man crusade for forceful "spokesmanship." Those letters proved his contention that there are *no weak words*—only *weak speakers*.

Chapter Nine

A Most Colossal Crest

Suddenly, in 1929, Lawrence Brings was in his early thirties. Only ten years before, the United States had shipped millions of young men across the Atlantic to fight the German Kaiser in World War I. That was an age when ladies' skirts swished along the ground.

During the ensuing decade, history picked up speed. In 1929, "flappers" wore an earlier version of the mini-skirt and acted emancipated. Somehow, the men didn't get the message.

That was the year of the Stock Market Crash that would catapult the country into the Great Depression, but Lawrence and Ethel Brings would be too busy to sit around wringing their hands, even though their checking account had been frozen in the bank.

While Ethel and Marianne worked long days in the office and classrooms, Lawrence was in and out of the college—teaching, advising and lecturing. Here, there and everywhere! No teachers' institute in the Upper Midwest was considered complete without his presence. He was recognized as a "teacher's teacher." They wanted to hear him discuss "Methods of Teaching Reading in the Grades." They were interested in knowing how to cope with "Stammering, Stuttering and Lisping." "How to Coach Plays" continued to be a popular topic with Speech and English teachers.

Play-coaching was a major course in the Northwestern College of Speech Arts. Because he had created a lively drama department, the president of the college would be heading toward a new crest before the "Roaring Twenties" were over—without realizing the significance of the first small ripples.

Lawrence had built up a fine library of plays—mostly Samuel French publications—at the speech school. "Sometimes I would hunt for a certain play I needed," he said, "and there wouldn't be a copy left on the shelves! It became apparent that too many teachers were borrowing copies and forgetting to return them."

Professor Brings solved the expensive problem of his disappearing plays by deciding to sell them. "I sent a seventy-five-dollar order to Samuel French in New York and offered to act as a midwestern representative," he recalls. "Then I bought a stack of *penny* postcards, at a time when a penny could buy something, and sent notices to schools and teachers. In no time I was swamped with orders and had to rush a quick S.O.S. to Samuel French. During the first three months, the new 'sideline' grossed more than fifteen hundred dollars."

Evidently there was much more to the play business than giving dramatic readings and coaching teachers and students. Larry Brings had already done some creative editing, adapting plays to accommodate smaller casts and scenery limitations in producing the Chautauqua plays—but he had never considered becoming a playwright or competing with Samuel French as a publisher.

The future was cresting upward in earnest when Professor Brings went to Iowa to keep a lecture engagement. There he met a fascinating man named Dr. Homer B. Hulbert who had served for twenty years as advisor to the Emperor of Korea—when Korea still had emperors. After listening to Hulbert's lecture about "The Menace of Japan," LMB signed him up for the Northwestern Lecture Bureau which was another sideline of the Speech College.

On his way back to Springfield, Mass., Dr. Hulbert was offered a ride to the nearest rail connection in his Model T, allowing them plenty of time for conversation. During that trip, he learned that Dr. Hulbert had written a play called "The Mummy Bride." The plot sounded good, so Lawrence offered to buy the amateur acting and publishing rights for $150 after reading the manuscript. He hired a printer to print it, and sold copies at 50 cents each and production rights for a royalty of ten dollars a performance. He still beams with satisfaction when he says, "I made a net profit of five hundred dollars in royalties the first year—and still owned the rights to the play."

He could be even more smug about his profitable relationship with the man who wrote "Tiger House." A future career as a play publisher began to loom large when Lawrence went to see the Bainbridge Players, a Minneapolis stock company, in their weekly repertoire of plays. One of the stars was a young man named Robert St. Clair. St. Clair had grown up in a Canadian theatrical family that included young Boris Karloff and Pearl White of "Perils of Pauline" among its touring troupers.

Going to the theater and meeting actors was a favorite "postman's holiday" for the man who taught speech and drama every day. He went backstage to visit with the debonair Robert St. Clair and enjoyed chatting with him about show business. When St. Clair mentioned that he had written a play called "Tiger House," Lawrence Brings pricked up his ears. "I'd like to read it," he said.

He took the manuscript home, and the next night he offered St. Clair five hundred dollars for the publishing and amateur rights. Five hundred dollars, when he was crowding his life with lecture tours to keep the speech college afloat! Again, he was listening to his intuition, playing a hunch, taking a chance —on the spur of the moment.

After "Tiger House" started rolling off the press, Lawrence put a twenty-five dollar royalty a performance on the production.

" 'Tiger House' made us!" he exclaimed, the memory still blazing brightly in his mind. This was the upward surge that propelled him into the play publishing business—and toward even more tantalizing challenges.

Before LMB realized that Robert St. Clair would be such a "gold mine," the young actor sent another manuscript to him. He added this plaintive plea, "If you buy this play, I can get married!" Lawrence Brings paid two hundred dollars for the play, and

Robert St. Clair, after marrying his actress sweet-heart, Kathryn Prather, in Michigan, drove to California. St. Clair would become a "household word" in the Brings family—for more reasons than anyone could imagine in 1929.

"Tiger House," which netted its publisher many thousands of dollars in royalties over the years, gave the new enterprise the boost it needed. Naturally Lawrence Brings held its author in high regard. The prolific Mr. St. Clair wrote between 200 and 250 plays, and a majority of them were published by The Northwestern Press.

The new play-publishing company was christened The Northwestern Press. The actual processing was done by a Minneapolis printing company for more than twenty years. Knowing Lawrence, we can be certain that he took an educational interest in the technical side of the business—the work of the type-setters, pressmen and printing tradesmen—just as he had done at the *St. Peter Free Press.*

At first, Lawrence Brings was publishing dozens of plays, then hundreds during the 1930s and 1940s. The launching of The Northwestern Press in 1929 was a hazardous adventure at that time in history. The Great Depression would soon cause businesses to fail and pennies to be scarce, but amateur theatri-cals would raise the spirits of people who needed to forget their woes for a few hours. Admission prices were low, and it was thrilling to act in plays—or to watch relatives and friends perform on com-munity stages.

From the very first, Lawrence Brings was doubly qualified to write advertising for a catalog and promotion brochures. He had spoken at many schools and colleges and had met thousands of interested teachers. These would be the first recipients of his brochures, flyers and play pamphlets. The market was waiting, but he must stimulate the demand for his particular publications.

Practically all his life he had been a salesman—using all his ingenuity to sell newspapers, church magazines and books, and aluminum kitchenware. He had sold himself as a lecturer with unusual talents, as well as a speech teacher with an enlightened philosophy for his students. His experience as a performer had taught him to be imaginative in arousing the attention of prospective audiences. He knew what they wanted—and what amateur actors could handle with haphazard stage facilities.

So, he was a salesman again, and this time he was selling plays. He "knew his territory" thoroughly, because he had kept learning as he taught. In reading manuscripts for amateur theatricals, Lawrence Brings could visualize the young actors—the blatant extroverts who could carry the leading roles, the introverts who were forcing themselves to be brave, and the ones with stage fright who wanted to run before the curtain came up. He knew he had to find plays that would be fun to perform, that would keep even the most bashful performer from "freezing."

Just as he had been known for "clean" speeches that would never embarrass his audience, the President of The Northwestern Press who was still in charge of the Northwestern College of Speech Arts —chose play scripts that would entertain the Great

American Family. Dramas featuring drinking, smoking or obscene material were "banned by Brings."

Humorous plots, rich in innocent mischief, received top consideration. Sophisticated comedy was sometimes suitable, but serious drama usually demanded seasoned actors—of which there were very few in the average high school. As every student knows, a well-plotted mystery could always pack the auditorium for the class play.

Lawrence Brings kept all those factors in mind while he was accepting a few and rejecting a great many scripts that were submitted. Since he was still "testing" the market, he took a brief fling at the classics, publishing an adaptation of a Robert Browning work. "It sold two copies," he says ruefully. "I finally bundled up the rest of the edition, and Keith took it to his school paper sale."

In addition to all his former chores at the speech college and on the lecture circuit, Lawrence was now a manuscript reader. Ethel often assisted him by eliminating the ones that lacked merit or were written in longhand, but the publishing business had multiplied her own office duties.

Since they were working so hard, you would think they were wallowing in prosperity, but buying those early scripts and paying the printers were costly investments. There was even more belt-tightening around the Northwestern Press offices, with all the profits being pumped back into the company like blood transfusions.

Marianne still giggles when she reminisces about those penny-pinching days, when every paper clip or piece of string was precious. Wrapping paper and

string were hoarded, to be used again to wrap a ship-
ment. "Corrugated paper was considered priceless,"
says Marianne. "It was so scarce that it was hidden
in a special place and doled out in small pieces at
the request of people who desperately needed it to
wrap orders." She still shudders when she sees a
piece of corrugated paper in an office wastebasket.

Nowadays, damaged books are discarded or sold
for a few pennies. Back in the early 1930s, Ethel and
Marianne carefully *ironed* any wrinkled pages in
published plays before they were mailed out.

Growing up in that atmosphere, little Keith
learned frugality from his elders. In fact, he surpassed them. Marianne remembers the time when
Lawrence, Ethel and Keith went to the depot to take
the train to Duluth. At the ticket office, Lawrence
reached in his pocket and realized he had left his
billfold at home. The train was due, and Ethel's
parents would be expecting them. Ethel and Lawrence looked at each other in consternation.

"Don't you have any money, either?" Lawrence
asked his wife.

"No, I don't!" she told him, sounding pretty exasperated.

Then they became aware that nine-year-old Keith
was tugging at them, trying to get their attention.
"I have some money," he said.

Lawrence and Ethel exchanged amused glances.
The dear little fellow, they thought, he's trying to
be helpful with his pennies and nickels!

The little fellow dug his hand into his pocket and
pulled out a roll of bills—thirty dollars. On his birthday and at Christmas, he had received gifts of money

from his grandfather, and he had been "salting" it carefully away. His parents were happy to borrow that thirty dollars. It was more than enough for the train trip to Duluth!

As a former actress and speech teacher, Marianne continues to be an entertaining raconteur. She "re-creates reality" in technicolor tones, enabling the listener to see the scenes she depicts and feel involved in them. Her eyes sparkle with well-remembered pathos and humor as she reenacts all the roles in the unpublished script called "Lawrence's Ruptured Appendix."

From his story thus far, it would seem that Lawrence Brings was disgustingly healthy. Unlike most other mortals, he didn't have time to be sick. He had to meet with all those classes, and he had to keep all those lecture dates—in addition to everything else.

Only a critical disability could halt him in his tracks, and it happened while they were swamped with orders for plays. "Even when the doctor said he had a ruptured appendix, Larry didn't want to leave the office," Marianne recalls. Still protesting that he had too much work to do, he was rushed to the hospital. There he was, packed in ice for the emergency operation, still signing correspondence.

It was a feverish time for Ethel and Marianne, too, with all the business responsibilities falling on their shoulders. They were in a constant state of concern about Lawrence's condition, because a ruptured appendix was a major medical hazard forty years ago.

Ethel rushed to the hospital every day. "She usually seemed optimistic," Marianne remembers. "Then, one day, she came home in tears. She cried and cried—and couldn't stop."

Marianne tried to soothe her. "Lawrence is getting better. He's going to be all right."

"No, he isn't," Ethel wailed. "He's going to die!"

Marianne patted her shoulder. "Where did you get an idea like that? Of course he isn't."

"Yes, he is," Ethel gulped. "He has lost his will to live. He isn't reading his business mail!"

Perhaps Lawrence had actually reached a healthy point in his convalescence, learning to relax just a little for the grinding schedule ahead. Looking at the whole picture of his life, it seems that relaxing was the hardest "work" that Lawrence Brings ever could do—so he avoided it as though it were the plague.

The day after he was released from the hospital, he drove to Duluth to give a play performance at the Teachers College, standing on his feet before his audience for an hour and a half.

Soon Lawrence was back in the middle of the whole activity again, trying to make up for lost time. When he went on lecture tours in the 1930s, he was earning money to help finance Northwestern Press as well as the speech college. With his talent for salesmanship, he had a splendid opportunity to advertise his new enterprise. If he didn't remind his audiences that he was now in the play-publishing business, he wouldn't have been Lawrence Martin Brings.

As the orders for plays continued to increase, Lawrence realized he was heading The Northwestern Press in the right direction. The names of new playwrights were added to the list in the 1930s and 1940s, but the plays of Robert St. Clair kept stage curtains rising most briskly, far and wide.

The star playwright of The Northwestern Press had settled down in his wife's home state of California. When the Brings family took a trip to the West Coast, they visited at the home of Robert St. Clair. Keith Brings was about eleven at that time and totally indifferent about girls—even if they were as winsome as four-year-old Barbara St. Clair. Golden-haired "Barbie" obviously was smitten with the handsome blond lad and kept pestering him—much to Keith's annoyance.

Two years later, Barbara sent Keith this message, "Someday I'm going to marry you!" Keith considered it more of a threat than a love letter, but his mother put the note away among her souvenirs.

Remembering Robert St. Clair's valuable talents as a Northwestern Press playwright, Keith's father observed, "That would be a good way to keep the business in the family!"

Chapter Ten

Keith Makes a Decision

Young Keith Brings spent his boyhood in the middle of all the excitement and whirlwind activity of the speech college and play publishing business. From all the evidence, nobody asked him what he wanted to be when he grew up.

After finishing the elementary grades, Keith enrolled at Central High School. The family business had improved and he could afford to drive a car of his own—but he refused to be different than his classmates.

Upon graduating from Central High School in Minneapolis, Keith enrolled at Macalester College in St. Paul. His education was interrupted by "Greetings" from Uncle Sam and he was drafted into the army.

Private Keith Brings sailed for Europe with thousands of other young American servicemen. About the time they arrived, the war was nearing an end—but Keith could not rejoice in the aftermath. It was as grim and sickening as the battlefield to be among the liberators of a major concentration camp, where the bodies of Jewish victims were still stacked and waiting for the ovens. According to his father, Keith is still reluctant to talk about that nightmarish experience.

Private Brings was now an M.P. and served in General Patton's Honor Guard. The motion picture "Patton!" was of particular interest to Keith. After seeing General Patton twirling his revolver and studying the big map in his office, he can vouch for the accuracy with which the General's dramatic personality was portrayed by George C. Scott. At one point he remembers guarding a Nazi general when he went for an exercise walk.

One of the most coveted honors was the opportunity to attend three months of study at the University of Biarritz in France. Only two applicants from the Headquarters were accepted—and the other one was an officer. Keith studied speech and drama at Biarritz, and he was so successful that he was asked to stay on as an instructor and technical advisor for another six months. He enjoyed the total thirty-six weeks, becoming a member of the faculty until the army school was closed.

After that, he was transferred to the Air Corps Special Services and assigned as a Special Services Director at the Kaiser Wilhelm Theater in Weisbaden, Germany. He had seventy-five of Max Reinhardt's technicians working under him. They were all Nazis and treated him with chilly condescension. He sensed they were asking themselves, "What is this young kid doing, bossing us around?" When Keith happened to mention that his grandfather was married in beautiful Cologne Cathedral, they loosened up, became more friendly, and followed his directions in making stage scenery.

Lawrence still speaks with pride of Keith's service record. After his safe return to the United States and discharge, Larry and Ethel went to meet the young man in Chicago.

Keith went back to Macalester to finish earning his degree. He was active in drama and even had a job as an instructor in the theater department.

With that background, it might be a foregone conclusion that Keith would seek his fortune on Broadway. His parents had encouraged him to develop his talents, in everything from biology to theater arts, carefully refraining from trying to push him in any certain direction. The Brings enterprises were growing, but Keith would not be drawn into them by compulsion.

As an educator, Keith's father had always paid close attention to other people's aptitudes and talents. When someone applied for a job in his company, he asked, "What's your special interest?" Whether it was a truck farm in Little Canada or a play publishing business in Minneapolis, a son should not be expected to become the shadow of his father.

Lawrence Brings certainly knew from personal experience that his father couldn't "keep him down on the farm," and that applied to most of his brothers and sisters. One sister went to St. Cloud Teachers College and taught school for many years. Another attended commercial college and became a bookkeeper, which stretched into a lifetime career in her husband's business. A younger brother had always been interested in athletics in school. He worked for an aircraft company in California and also coached championship basketball teams until his retirement. Dorothy, who was the flower girl at Lawrence's wedding, trained herself for a business career and is now employed in a C.P.A. office.

Then there was Don, the brother who actually stayed "down on the farm" and made a fabulously successful business of it. Did Lawrence's hunger for education have much influence on his brothers and sisters?

"Not on Don!" he says with a twinkle of envy. "Don only went to high school for one year, and then he chose his own pathway to success. He worked for an easy-going produce dealer who specialized in selling flower plants and vegetables and was on the verge of bankruptcy most of the time. Don became a partner, and later he bought the whole business."

Seeing gold "in them thar onions," Don worked hard to build up a huge wholesale monopoly and establish himself as "Don Brings, the Onion King" of the Upper Midwest. That was the trademark on his trailer trucks. With only nine years of schooling, he had taught himself the fine art of marketing and advertising.

By the time he sold out to a young partner, Don's business and real estate investments in the Twin Cities area had made him a financial expert who could buy and sell almost anybody in sight—including his brother Lawrence—and he and his wife were spending their winters in Florida. And he did it all with vegetables and onions and one year of high school.

Comparing the frugality and hard labor of the old days with the achievements of his brothers and sisters—especially Don—Lawrence knew that each person must search out his own destiny. Let Keith measure the crests of his own horizon, at home or abroad.

As normal parents always do, Ethel and Lawrence sometimes wondered what Keith's decision would be. He was a young man with a tranquil personality who seemed to assume that his parents knew what he was thinking. One day, during his senior year at Macalester, he and his mother got into a short discussion one evening about job opportunities when Lawrence was at a meeting. With an opening like that, Ethel asked casually, "I don't suppose you are interested in going into the business?"

"What makes you think I'm not?" Keith answered decisively. "That's what I've always intended to do."

It was exciting news to Lawrence when reported to him by Ethel, and they were all choked up with delight. The Northwestern Press had taken a tremendous leap ahead after World War II, and Keith had already helped with play scripts and other business assignments. They needed him and his youthful point of view to give continuity to their expanding enterprises.

A few doubts still haunted Lawrence's mind. He knew that Keith had been offered a good job by a New York stage producer, and he thought he was considering the offer seriously. The father had a heart-to-heart talk with his only son and heir. Did he really want to go into the business, or did he feel obligated to carry on the family tradition?

"I want you to feel free to make your own decision," his father said, "with no strings attached. If you honestly want to be active in the company, tomorrow I'll arrange for you to have a ten percent interest."

Keith went to work in the Brings establishment after he graduated from college. He didn't expect special favors. For the first two years he worked as an addressing machine operator, learning the business as his parents had—from the ground up.

Even though he had spurned her advances as a youngster, the "Golden Girl" from California appeared completely exquisite to Keith when he became a young man. He discovered he wanted her to share his life. True to her predictions, Barbara St. Clair and Keith Brings were married in 1952.

Many years before, little Barbie had written Keith, "Someday I'm going to marry you." Ethel had saved the note, as though for future reference. After it was an accomplished fact, Ethel got out the "incriminating evidence" and took it along to a family theater party. She slipped the note to her daughter-in-law during a serious moment in the performance, when the audience was hushed. Barbara read it and whooped out loud—to the mystification of all the silent people in the theater.

Just as he had saved his money when he was a youngster, it was typical of Keith to send home all his pay checks when he was in the service, and the money had been deposited in trust for him.

After he and Barbara were married, Keith bought an apartment in a cooperative building. He and Barbara financed the purchase themselves, while Keith's father kept wondering if he should help. LMB decided it would be better for them to achieve independence in their own way, and he was proud to see that Keith shared his own respect for the value of money.

Lawrence still taught speech classes at Twin Cities seminaries and went on lecture tours once in awhile, but the Brings business interests changed considerably during World War II. The new company, with which Keith had chosen to cast his hopes for the future, would no longer include the Northwestern College of Speech Arts.

Around 1940, young men were concerned with enlistment, the draft, and service in the armed forces —rather than signing up for speech classes. Girls were going into munitions factories and other war work. The country was talking back to Hitler and Tojo with bullets, instead of trying to do business with them with words.

It had been a dynamic operation for sixteen years, and Lawrence and Ethel felt sad when they closed the doors of the speech school in 1940.

Lawrence concentrated mainly on the play publishing business after that, but he was always involved in a multitude of other church, civic and community programs.

As far as his business life was concerned, a grand climax—a crest that towered above them all—would be attained in 1944 in the city of Chicago, Illinois.

Chapter Eleven

The Great Merger

T. S. Denison & Company has been a magic name for generations, conjuring up visions of footlights gleaming, clowns dancing, and actors emoting in greasepaint and costumes to match the mood and scenery on thousands of stages all over the world.

Mellerdramas of Long Ago Moving to Modern Quarters was the title of a lengthy feature story by Gene Morgan, published in the *Chicago Daily News* on August 27, 1937. The famous old play publishing house was being transferred from South Wabash to North Wabash Avenue in Chicago, with scarcely a break in its operations.

On the eve of moving day, the reporter described the Denison offices as a sight-and-sound panorama of ". . . glistening glass showcases full of published plays, fast-moving silent typewriters, swiftly tiptoeing professional play readers, subdued piano strains rolling from a distant music room, serious-looking sales persons with spectacles, drama-conscious customers without spectacles—in fact, all of the modus operandi of the big business that supplies the needs of the nonprofessional stage."

This was the springboard to a kaleidoscopic land of fantasy that could turn small-town, workaday people into exciting heroes and heroines with the flick of a playscript. With enough hours of "play practice" in the average high school, it could create villains, comedians and spies.

T. S. Denison plays encircled the globe, wherever English was spoken. In 1937, before World War II, it was said that "the sun never sets on British soil." From the pinheads on a world map in the Denison office, it was obvious that teachers from Stratford-on-Avon to Khartoum, from Delhi to Peking to Singapore, kept ordering Denison plays for their students to perform. Even after World War II and the gradual collapse of colonialism, it could be said, "The moon always rises on T. S. Denison plays."

People often refer to T. S. Denison as though it were a company, instead of a flesh-and-blood person with a terrific imagination and a keen brain for business opportunities.

There are some similarities in the lives of Thomas S. Denison and Lawrence M. Brings, but Denison got a much earlier start. About twenty-five years before Larry Brings was even born, Tom Denison started his company in one room with one play, in 1876. Creative stimulus was in the air. That was the year when the country celebrated its one-hundredth birthday. The Civil War had just ended. Out in the West, General George Custer was leading his troops on a one-way expedition to the Little Big Horn.

In other words, Thomas Denison went into the play-writing business about one hundred years ago.

He, too, started as an educator, graduating from the State Normal College at Lebanon, Ohio, and teaching at Marengo and DeKalb, Illinois. In the process, he got a new-fangled notion that he could train his students to become amateur actors and put on a play. Denison studied the theatrical market and realized that the only plays available were "stuffy reprints" imported from England. Drawing room dramas from England—with butlers, maids, and ponderous dialogue—seemed ridiculous in a lusty young country of raw frontiers.

Thomas Denison decided to write a typical American play for American amateurs. In 1875, his theme certainly was contemporary. It was a Civil War melodrama entitled "Odds with the Enemy." Denison wrote two more plays in the next year, bought reprint rights to a few foreign dramas, and started sending out a small catalogue to former teaching associates—as Lawrence Brings would someday do.

The popularity of Thomas Denison's early plays endured for fifty years or more. Characterized by "straightforward dialogue, natural acting . . . and homely philosophy about small-town folks," they went into countless editions and sold hundreds of thousands of copies. So did the plays that Tom Denison bought from other writers to expand his list.

In addition to all the plays that poured out of his nimble brain, Denison published game books, skits for children, and educational books. By the time he "laid down his pen forever in 1911," the founder of T. S. Denison & Company was publishing an impressive catalogue, complete with plays, skits, dialogues, monologues, magic acts, costumes, and a variety of educational books for teachers.

In his 1937 story for the *Chicago Daily News*, Gene Morgan told of an interview with T. S. Denison's successor, a broad-shouldered man named Eben Holmes Norris who had joined the firm in 1892. His voice ringing with admiration for his departed colleague, Mr. Norris declared, "He was a man of great foresight. He foresaw his plays lasting decades, not a few weeks or months on Broadway and the road. He avoided topical slang. He devised situations and pictured characters which are universal and lasting in appeal. He wrote on the basis of good common sense, avoiding the false dramatics of impassioned artificialities of his period." Above all, Mr. Norris emphasized, "He believed in clean humor."

Since Lawrence Brings of Minneapolis subscribed wholeheartedly to the Denison-Norris tradition of wholesome drama and clean humor, he and Norris were kindred souls when they met at educators' and publishers' conventions. The Minneapolis man visited the T. S. Denison establishment when he was in Chicago and was fascinated with the operations of the fine old company. He enjoyed listening to the stories Mr. Norris told about his half-century as one of the two owners of T. S. Denison & Company.

The Northwestern Press in Minneapolis was smaller and newer than T. S. Denison, but they shared the same business interests. Brings and Norris could be helpful to each other. "There was some talk about an affiliation," Lawrence remembers. "I was seriously considering buying into the Chicago firm."

While he was still measuring the height of that challenge in his mind, Lawrence Brings learned that the elderly Mr. Norris had passed away. Now what would happen to T. S. Denison? That question led Lawrence Brings to make some inquiries. "I learned that the estate was in probate, so I got in touch with the lawyer who was handling it. Evidently the only heir, Mrs. Norris, wasn't interested in continuing the business.

There was every possibility that competitors would develop an interest in the proud old Denison Company—when they learned it could be purchased at a very reasonable figure. Larry Brings knew he would have to reach the dizzy heights of this transaction in one quick leap, or not at all. After a couple of breathless days of examining the Denison financial statements and talking to Chicago business people, he made a bid to the probate court and the offer was accepted. "I didn't even have time to go back to Minneapolis and discuss it with Ethel," he recalls.

There was one thing he noticed in going through the Denison files. No wonder he was able to get such a bargain! It was obvious that Mr. Norris, in his later years, had been more preoccupied with office procedures than with selling plays and books. Sales were not as high as they should have been, but Mr. Norris had kept meticulous track of every little transaction. There were drawers and drawers of stencil record cards, with complete information about each customer—even those who had only ordered a fifty-cent item. Everything was indexed and cross-indexed, with an elaborate system of filing cabinets to keep a large office force busy. Now it all belonged to Lawrence Martin Brings—who could make his own decisions about changing office procedures.

Just like that, Lawrence Brings had gained the summit of the most formidable crest on the horizon. It was there, and he had climbed it with all the guts and gall of the poor truck farmer's son who had decided to go to high school, to college, and into business for himself in the big city.

Now he was suddenly in a bigger business, in a much bigger city—Carl Sandburg's "City of Big Shoulders." For the Minneapolis man, this was the "business adventure" to top them all! His motto might have been: "Nobody promotes a man. A man must promote himself."

When he purchased T. S. Denison & Company in 1944, L. M. Brings was past his middle forties—but he had kept that old mental "bounce," that yeasty combination of compulsion and propulsion. While most men are hanging onto the same old job at that age, cherishing their "seniority" and looking forward to relaxing on their pensions, Brings was still gambling on a tempting new challenge with all the zest of a Gustavus senior.

Ethel was pleased to hear about the acquisition of T. S. Denison. After almost twenty-five years of marriage and business partnership, she trusted her husband's good judgment. When their twenty-fifth wedding anniversary arrived, Larry wrote her a special letter in which he expressed his appreciation for her devotion as a wife and business helpmate. To celebrate the occasion, Ethel was urged to select "a mink coat of her choice."

World War II ended in 1945, and business was great. Lawrence Brings, whose working days were never long enough for all he had to do, was commuting back and forth to Chicago in addition to supervising the Minneapolis firm. Sometimes he considered merging the double operation in one city, but there was some advantage in owning companies in two different states. The idea of expansion appealed to his imagination, and it was good business to have access to theatrical markets and playwrights in different sections of the country.

Because of its Chicago connections, the company kept receiving splendid publicity from the heart of the national newspaper world. John Chapman, a major Broadway play critic, saluted T. S. Denison in the Theater-Music Section of the *Chicago Sunday Tribune* on Sept 21, 1947. Pointing out that "This country produces about a half million amateur theatrical performances each year," Mr. Chapman added benevolently, "They aren't as professional as the ones in the cities, but they afford a good time for everybody concerned."

Remember when Lawrence Brings ordered seventy-five dollars' worth of plays from Samuel French, back around 1927? In 1947, Mr. Chapman coupled Samuel French and T. S. Denison of Minneapolis in the same sentence. By that time, of course, T. S. Denison and Lawrence Brings were synonymous.

Mr. Chapman had just received the latest Denison catalog and described it as a "fascinating collection." It inspired him to predict: "Out of catalogs such as Denison's and French's will come soon some of the best actors of the next generation. Some kid cast for a role in 'The Absent Minded Bridegroom' . . . may show a genius for play acting and may become the Alfred Lunt or Lynn Fontanne of the 1950s or 1960s."

Mr. Chapman had seen them all, and he thought the Denison plays deserved "more kindly consideration" than a certain 1947 Broadway production which "was not even decently amateurish."

The advertising blurbs were typical of Lawrence Brings. The Denison play catalog, according to the Broadway critic, "makes enchanting reading because it is so all-fired optimistic." Each play got a "rave notice." There was "The Adorable Imp," which was described as "a laugh riot in three acts." Another play was "an uproar of farcical fun." And hardly a play coach could resist this rollicking rhetoric: "One riotously funny situation follows another in rapid succession."

Some of the riotously funny situations in T. S. Denison comedies included a cat having kittens on a mink coat in one play, and an old hen laying an egg in a lady's "ritzy" hat in another. Pity the amateur property man who wanted to be authentic, scouring the town for newborn kittens!

The catalog stressed the philosophy that Lawrence Brings had developed during more than twenty-five years of play coaching and publishing. The productions were designed to rank with the best professional plays, "the chief difference being that in selecting them certain limitations of the amateur's stage facilities have been kept in mind . . ."

In the 1947 Denison catalog, highest-priced plays could be bought for a royalty of ten dollars, plus sixty cents a copy for each character and the director. Some were royalty free. These included "Damsels in Distress," which was described as "a farce so screamingly funny that it practically plays itself." Perfect for amateurs!

Mr. Chapman reached the conclusion that the amateur play business "is not peanuts." He considered it "a big business and not to be sneered at by the likes of me. Denison, in making a pitch for 'home talent' plays, says they provide a good way of developing outstanding dramatic talent and they will be highly appreciated in communities where there is no professional spoken drama available."

The Broadway critic, who was considered an "intellectual" in theatrical circles, was no snob. He ended his story on this highly agreeable note: " 'A good spoken play, well produced,' says the catalog, 'is the most satisfying evening's entertainment ever devised for an educated community.' Okay, Denison!"

The Theater-Music Section of that issue of the *Chicago Sunday Tribune* is a journey back to our distant yesterdays. In the fall of 1947, girls were pictured wearing their skirts four inches below the knee. You could go to the legitimate theater in Chicago and see Tallulah Bankhead in Noel Coward's "Private Lives." If you wanted to see a movie, a younger Lucille Ball was playing in a film called "Lured," and Betty Grable was featured in "Mother Wore Tights."

That entertainment section of the *Chicago Trib* was packed with news about records, fiction, radio programs and movies. Still, you get an uneasy feeling that something is missing. Of course—television! Where are all those pages of program listings, and all the "human interest stories" about Matt Dillon, Archie Bunker, and Desi Arnez, Jr.—who was far from being born when his mother was filming "Lured"? Still in the future. In six or seven years, someone in every block would have a TV set, and all the neighborhood kids would gather around it to cheer for "The Lone Ranger." For better or for worse, it is difficult now to imagine an age when Americans didn't have television.

Would TV cause rumblings and palpitations in the theatrical business—professional and amateur? Would a good spoken play, on a local stage, still be "the most satisfying evening's entertainment?" In the 1940s and well into the 1950s, there were no worries about TV competition. Amateur acting was going full blast, and drama coaches were ordering scripts as fast as they could be printed.

Before they could be printed, it was necessary to find appropriate plays, musical comedies, sketches, vaudeville acts, readings, assembly programs, pep meeting suggestions, skits and radio programs. A good playwright was almost as difficult to find as a snowflake in July. It took a special kind of talent to concoct "riotous" dialog, keep the plot moving at a swift pace and diagram all the stage directions so the amateur actors wouldn't exit by the wrong door or trip over the props.

Lawrence, Ethel and Keith might burn the midnight oil scanning hundreds of manuscripts before they struck just one vein of "gold"—a clean, clear, amusing story with enough excitement to keep the actors stimulated and the audience entertained. They were glad they had a number of "reliables" like Robert St. Clair and Jay Tobias to keep filling their play production lists.

Costuming was an important "sideline," with Northwestern Press and Denison doing a flourishing business in wigs, stage accessories and minstrel show outfits. Even today, if you go snooping at the back of the new publishing plant, you will find some boxes of wigs—fuzzy reminders of a yesteryear when heroines wore longer tresses than the heroes did.

Chapter Twelve

His Great Adventure

Lawrence Martin Brings had become an important businessman by the time he was in his early fifties. After the purchase of the T. S. Denison Company, his dramatic strides toward success were often chronicled in Twin Cities news stories and columns.

No Horatio Alger story is complete without a human interest angle. Reporters could say, in 1950, "Here is a man who owns four publishing companies. Undoubtedly he is making money in a business that appeals to the imagination — amateur theatrical productions. But what kind of a human being is he? What are his hobbies when he isn't at the office?"

When Lawrence Brings went to visit Sweden in 1950, the public learned about one of his many "spare-time hobbies" — the Folke Bernadotte Memorial Foundation, named in honor of the United Nations mediator who was assassinated in Jerusalem in 1948. The Minnesota publisher took with him this letter, emblazoned with the Seal of Minnesota—

137

"L'Etoil du Nord"—and signed by Governor Luther W. Youngdahl:

To Whom It May Concern: Please be advised that I have known Lawrence M. Brings for many years. He is one of the outstanding citizens of Minnesota.

We are proud of him as an ambassador of good-will from Minnesota to Sweden. Any courtesies you may extend to him will be sincerely appreciated.

Some mighty impressive people were concerned with the visit to Stockholm of Dr. Carlson and Mr. Brings from Gustavus Adolphus College. Everyone was aware that Lawrence Brings was being saluted as one of the organizers of the Folke Bernadotte Foundation.

An information conference, which attracted leading Swedish-American educators, was arranged for March 24, 1950. Among the participants were Mr. Olaf H. Lamm, former Swedish Consul General in New York, chairman of the board of the graduate school for English-speaking students at the University of Stockholm; Dr. Eric C. Bellquist, head of the information department of the American Embassy; Mr. Thorsten Brandel, first secretary of the Ministry for Foreign Affairs; Mrs. Adele Heilborn, director of the Swedish-American Foundation and member of the board of the graduate school for English-speaking students at the University of Stockholm; Dag Hammarskjold of the Foreign Office, and other notables with lengthy titles and important positions.

There was a memorable morning with His Royal Highness, the Crown Prince of Sweden, on March 28. On that same day, they also had an interview with Earl Marshall Ekeberg. The next day they sat with Prime Minister Erlander in the Swedish Parliament. The final day featured a formal luncheon with educators at Operakillaren, a meeting with Mr. Weijne who was Minister of Education, a conference at the Swedish Institute, and a press conference in the evening.

In his wildest dreams as a boy on the truck farm, did little Larry ever foresee such moments as those —to travel across the Atlantic Ocean and be welcomed by a future king, a prime minister and a future Secretary-General of the United Nations, and educators of international prestige?

If he had been in a hurry to travel, he could have gone to Scandinavia as a sales representative of the Aluminum Company of America when he finished at Gustavus. Now he knew he had made a wiser choice—building a solid foundation of achievement at home in various fields of activity.

He had been building a business, yes, but the congregation at Central Lutheran Church in Minneapolis knew that he had been building something more enduring, more spiritually satisfying. He had poured his talents for forensics, financial organization, and teaching into a magnificent labor of love that would produce visible and invisible treasures for a small church, founded on the faith of twelve families in 1919.

Such a small beginning—in a rented church, without synodical guidance or a minister of their own. Perhaps that is what stirred the imagination of the young speech teacher, back in 1923. Lawrence Brings has always been fascinated with success stories that started with humble beginnings.

Spiritually, Central Lutheran was a success from the day that the first twelve men gathered together at the Odin Club to plan for the future in 1917, the year when the United States entered World War I.

Many years later our Minneapolis publisher would look back over all those decades and write:

> This is the story of a church. In itself, this is not important. It is more significant that it is the romantic story of a great church. They who founded it were men of vision, those who followed were rich in faith. The cornerstone upon which the structure rested was service to others.

It was typical of Lawrence Brings to think of the miracle of Central Lutheran Church as a romantic story, an inspiring Christian drama with all the ingredients of a Twentieth Century classic: great people and small people who were alike in the eyes of the Lord, good fortune and misfortune, vales of tears and peaks of rejoicing, abundant harvests in God's vineyard, and bleak shadows of catastrophe to heighten the suspense.

When Lawrence Brings reviewed the early years of Central Lutheran Church, his rhetoric soared with noble phrases. The first chapter was titled, "In the Beginning—A Great Adventure." The subtitle was from Carlyle, "The beginning remains always the most notable event."

The history of this Lutheran landmark could not be written overnight, and there will be many other "great adventures" during its existence, but its original purpose was most significant. "Unique" is the word that is often used. Those first twelve men recognized the "unique need" for a downtown church "with a mission of service."

Minneapolis was the major metropolis of Minnesota and the upper midwest in 1917, with people pouring into the heart of the city from foreign lands and rural communities to seek job opportunities. Most of them ended their journeys at the railroad depot and looked for lodgings in nearby rooming houses and apartment buildings that had risen like rabbit hutches. Many of the newcomers were young people from the farm, and later there were young veterans from World War I battlefields—freed from the anchor of home ties and home churches. Freedom often brought loneliness in drab rooms, with consequent temptations to stray from "the straight and narrow" of parental teachings.

The founders of the new church had faith in the good intentions of those young people. They were also mindful of older citizens who might suffer hardship in getting to distant churches. Central Lutheran, in the crowded heart of the city, would throw wide its doors to welcome all people, "regardless of race, creed or color."

The church would not only minister to spiritual needs, it would be deeply concerned with "the temporal ills that man is heir to" and with "the friendly social intercourse which is so much an inherent part of the lives of a free and happy people."

The first pastor, the Rev. Dr. J. A. O. Stub, was a jewel among spiritual leaders. Enlightened, eminent, and eloquent—he could have chosen to serve in any prestigious Lutheran church in the country. Instead, he answered the call of this unpretentious congregation in a rented church in downtown Minneapolis. The salary was no attraction, but he was drawn by the dreams and visions of twelve courageous Christian men and their families. It was a challenge worthy of a good shepherd.

Lawrence Brings described Pastor Stub as "a masterful organizer." Shortly after his installation on Palm Sunday in 1919, the church was filled to capacity on Easter Sunday — only a week later! Soon Pastor Stub was recruiting volunteers to seek funds for the church budget, and the pledges surpassed the amount needed for 1920.

Less than a year after his arrival at Central Lutheran Church, the congregation met with Pastor Stub and authorized the purchase of the rented church property. In one year, the congregation had grown from twelve families to 220—a grand total of 581 individual members! Dr. Stub did not take credit for this phenomenon. He looked into the upturned faces of the congregation and spoke a psalm of thanksgiving: "This is the Lord's doing. It is marvelous in our eyes."

Campaigns for new members marched hand in hand with budget appeals to keep the fledgling church afloat. There were frequent setbacks, but Central managed to pay off most of the cost of its original building in four years—while still contributing generously to foreign missions and domestic needs.

Wherever the members of Central Lutheran went, they sang the praises of their church. They were ready to make disciples of anyone who would listen to the fascinating story of Central's brave concept and its unique purposes.

Oliver Prestholdt and several other members of Central Lutheran Church were enrolled in one of Professor Brings' speech classes, back in late August, 1923. It was natural that Mr. Prestholdt, one of the twelve "founding fathers," should carry the glad tidings of Central into the classroom.

Mr. Prestholdt had been a wise judge of the speech teacher's leadership qualities and his ability to "communicate" his Christian principles. Christianity had influenced the development of Lawrence Brings' personality since early childhood. Later, he had preached his love of Jesus Christ, with eloquence and fervor, from church pulpits. He believed that a minister should glorify the Blessed Trinity as though every Sunday were a new Pentecost. Theology fascinated him, and he enjoyed exploring minds of biblical characters and sharing his discoveries with an attentive audience.

Lawrence, working with the pastor, wrote of their joint endeavors, "Pastor Stub regarded the Sunday School as the great missionary agency of Central Lutheran Church." It started with the Cradle Roll, reached a climax in confirmation, and leveled off in a teen-age plateau with the Young People's League—but actually the "Sunday School influence" permeated all age groups in one way or another.

No Sunday School child was neglected, not even those who came from "unchurched homes" in the vicinity. All were remembered on their birthdays. Each teacher visited her pupils in their homes, and parents were invited to attend Sunday School classes and participate in special exercises. Since the teachers were volunteers, all this personal attention was made possible by setting the pupil-teacher ratio at ten to one. Central Lutheran has adhered quite closely to that ideal program through the years.

Building firm foundations has always been a major ambition in the life of Lawrence Brings— as a family man, a church member, a businessman, and a civic leader. Just skimming the surface was not enough.

When Lawrence became a member of Central Lutheran Church, it was a one hundred percent commitment—in all phases of church life, as well as the Sunday School. He delighted in hearing stories about the resourcefulness that was already apparent to the congregation. On one occasion when money was needed, picture postcards of Central Lutheran were printed and sold for five cents each. They became such "best sellers" that additional printings had to be ordered.

The miracle of Central Lutheran could often be traced to the ingenious spirit of the congregation, with everyone putting his shoulder to the wheel during those early years. When the men's club was first organized, the members pushed ahead so enthusiastically that they found themselves over $5,000 in arrears. They hired a concert group for $500, promoted the event with fervor, and took in $6,400—

to wipe out the debt in one evening, with a little extra for their treasury.

Lawrence Brings was very much at home among people who refused to be conquered by trials and tribulations, because he had always been a little more resourceful and ingenious than anybody.

From all accounts, an atmosphere of good fellowship prevailed at Central from the beginning. Lawrence and Ethel became involved immediately, often entertaining Sunday School teachers and other church groups at "socials" in their Speech School.

The congregation was already overflowing the seating capacity of the rented church by 1921. Four years later, Lawrence and Ethel Brings were among the very active members when this "exultant communication" went forth: "The great campaign for a new church is on!"

Turning that vision into reality was easier said than done, but it was an age when mighty deeds and hard work were respected—and expected.

As the original church kept drawing worshippers far beyond its capacity, Dr. Stub and the congregation often debated whether the structure should be enlarged or if the time had come to build a large, new edifice.

As always, the pastor took some abuse for his "extravagant dreams" of expansion of the church property, starting with the acquisition of a nearby plot of land for $24,000—and peaking upward to an awesome commitment of $675,000 to finance the magnificent sanctuary that would rise upon it. Dr. Stub also was criticized for his ecumenical contacts with other denominations and clergymen of other faiths. As might be expected, Lawrence Brings would someday write with admiration of this saintly man who was ahead of his time!

Under Pastor Stub's inspired leadership, the congregation set to work, turning pennies into dollars—and multiplying them many thousandfold. Faith in the future of a "Greater Central Lutheran Church" was demonstrated by contributions, pledges, and the "Coolidge confidence" of the business community in long-term mortgage bonds. It was a time of prosperity, without inflation.

LMB described the willing workers at Central as "Doers as well as dreamers," citing the zealous cooperation from many organizations inside the church. There were countless church dinners served by the women—a bountiful meal for as little as fifty cents back in the 1920s! There were always dozens of little economies, while nothing of religious significance was neglected. They even paid salaries to an organist and a director of music.

The story is told in detail in *What God Hath Wrought,* Lawrence Brings' fascinating history of Central Lutheran's first fifty years. There are breathtaking descriptions of the architectural masterpiece —"a great Gothic cathedral, a storied structure of stone, classic in outline, beautiful in form, a fitting monument to the faith of its founders."

In *What God Hath Wrought,* the new sanctuary soars to life in phrases of sacred grandeur—from its "random ashlar" stonework to its graceful copper spire with pinnacles and gargoyles.

On a cold Christmas Day in 1927, we follow Lawrence Brings and the wide-eyed congregation into the spacious main floor of the Gothic cathedral where 1,750 worshippers could be seated. Our eyes are drawn to the dominant point of vision—the plain bronze cross rising in majestic simplicity above an altar made of huge slabs of Colfax sandstone. There are glowing descriptions of the gallery which could seat 1,500, the vaulted Gothic ceiling, the cathedral windows, the choir pews, and the baptismal and wedding chapels. The elaborate pulpit and lectern are given special attention, with explanations of the symbolic significance of the hand-carved panels.

Truly the people could gasp and exclaim, "What God Hath Wrought!" It was a miracle of miracles, dwarfing Lindbergh's solo flight to Paris in that same year. As Minneapolis banker Clifford Sommer said recently, "It doesn't seem possible that twelve men could try to organize a congregation in 1917—and build such a magnificent church only ten years later!"

Dr. Stub and the congregation had worked tirelessly for that moment, and they knew their labors were far from finished. They would continue with a renewed spirit of jubilation, emphasizing Central's "mission of service" above all—but ever mindful of the huge bonded indebtedness that must be lifted from the vaulted heights of their beloved cathedral-church.

Then the Coolidge years of prosperity and optimism collided with the Great Depression of the 1930s, but Central Lutheran was rich in fellowship and membership. Superintendent Brings could count 700 pupils enrolled in the Sunday School, with 58 instructors. There were organizations and activities for everyone — The Women's Guild, the Sunday

Evening Fireside Hour with Mr. Brings as chairman for seven years, The Girls' Club, The Men's Club, The Young People's Club, The Nurses' Club, the Teachers' Club, Boys' and Girls' Clubs which included Boy and Girl Scout troops, and any number of affiliated activists who were dedicated to Central's motto of "Service to Others."

They had a beautiful church and a beautiful congregation—but not enough beautiful money. Pastor Stub must have prayed more than he slept, when interest payments were larger than the year's income.

There were brave attempts to raise money. Lawrence Brings noted that they used Exodus 35:22 as a guideline when the banks were closed in 1933, appealing to the congregation to donate "pieces of gold or silver jewelry, broken or whole, old spectacle frames, watches, trinkets—anything containing precious metal . . ."

But only a major miracle could save Central from bankruptcy, at a time when large businesses were going broke and many people were without jobs and money.

The miracle did happen. One "mysterious" gentleman took it upon himself to save the church, devoting countless days and nights over a period of seven years to the supreme effort. He described his technique as "simple," but most mortals would consider it fantastically complicated. Even the thought of wrestling with a bonded indebtedness of $675,000 would make most of us dizzy.

This "miracle worker" sent letters to all the bondholders, almost a thousand of them, offering to buy their Central securities at a discount. That was a stroke of genius, because the anxious bondholders were likely to take what they could get. After he purchased a bond, our money wizard would approach a member of Central Lutheran and propose that he buy it. This was an individual undertaking without the knowledge and authorization of the church's officers.

That, of course, is a clue to the identity of the man who saved Central. In a spirit of levity it might be said that Lawrence Brings would know where the money was—even during and after the most miserable Depression in the Twentieth Century.

Although the story of Central Lutheran would have been quite different without his dynamic crusade to rescue the church from disaster, the erstwhile Sunday School Superintendent insisted on remaining anonymous in *What God Hath Wrought*. Under cross-examination by the author of this biography, he admitted that he masterminded the whole blessed business—for the glory of God and the perpetuation of Central Lutheran Church.

Perhaps this was the reason Lawrence Brings had not felt "called" to the ministry. The Lord was saving his talents for this "loud, clear call" in later years. As a layman, it was right and proper for him to operate as a "hard-nosed money man" in the interests of the church. Such blatant financial activity might have been considered "unseemly" for a pastor.

Somehow Lawrence Brings got those bonds into the hands of members who could buy them at the discount price immediately. Over the years, as the church paid off the full value of the bonds, Larry developed another bright idea. He persuaded many of the owners to donate their bonds to the Central Lutheran Church Endowment Fund—another of his projects to make the church self-sufficient and provide a strong bulwark against any future depressions or threats of insolvency. In the same frame of mind, he later launched the campaign to raise money for Gustavus Adolphus College and a number of other philanthropic beneficiaries.

In addition to various Central Lutheran activities during the bond-buying years, Lawrence was President of the Men's Club in 1938 and 1939. Marianne remembers that he increased the membership by leaps and bounds, exceeding 400 men—with some assistance from her. After she got home from the office at night, she would spend time calling members who could not be reached in the daytime to remind them of meetings. There was a typical "Brings touch" to those depression-era festivities. The winner of the door prize always had to bring the door prize for the next meeting.

Chapter Thirteen

Always Forging Ahead

By the time Pastor Stub's health began to fail and he chose Dr. Elmer S. Hjortland as his successor in 1945, it was apparent that Lawrence Brings had set Central Lutheran Church firmly on the road to financial stability.

Pastor Stub had been an inspiration to L. M. Brings and all the members of the congregation. Oliver Prestholdt, who had worked closely with the pastor through the long span of years from 1919 to 1945, saluted the distinguished churchman with these words, "He took his trials and tribulations admirably, and when he passed on, I joined with others to say, 'A great man in Israel has fallen!'" That glorious tribute would be immortalized in the pages of *What God Hath Wrought.*

After this brief review of Larry Brings' fabulous achievements on behalf of Central Lutheran Church from 1923 to mid-century, we are back where we left off—ready for new slants on his personality. About the time Lawrence went to Sweden, he was also going everywhere else around the countryside! The *Minneapolis Tribune* and the *Greater Gustavus*

Quarterly honored him as "The Man Who Came to Dinner"—because he was perpetually in demand on the knife and fork circuit.

According to the editor's note in the *Gustavus Quarterly*, "There's an old saying that if you want to get a job done, ask the busiest person you know. That's exactly the reason the Greater Gustavus Association chose Lawrence Brings, '20, to head the Student Union Building campaign." Most of the following material first appeared in the *Minneapolis Tribune:*

"A man who can't call his lunch hour his own is Lawrence M. Brings, play publisher, Rotarian, Lutheran, college alumnus, club president, Usadian, Coast Guard Leaguer, and fisherman.

"Monday, through Friday, Brings is booked solid for luncheon meetings.

"Monday it's the Rotary Club program meeting; Tuesday it's the Lutheran Luncheon Club; Wednesday it's the Lakeshore Athletic Club; Thursday it's the Usadian Club, and Friday finds him at the main Rotarian luncheon.

"Brings doesn't do much better in the evenings. Last week he wasn't home for dinner once.

"As the chairman of the board of trustees of Central Lutheran Church he finds board meetings and special committee meetings awaiting his presence in the evening. Several committees of the Lakeshore Athletic Club, of which he is president, call him out at night during the month.

"He is general chairman of the Gustavus Adolphus College alumni campaign to raise $500,000 for a student union building, and organizational meetings now keep his date book crowded."

He was so efficient that he even managed a little time for fun and recreation in his cruiser on Lake Minnetonka. The reporter explained that "His summer fishing group meets during the winter to show movies of the members' fishing trips. Last year he was district commander of the second district of the Coast Guard League, and he is active in the local chapter . . .

"Brings is noted not only for the number of meetings he attends, but also for the fact that he has a remarkable memory for names and faces, and likes to introduce members and guests without resorting to notes.

"Lawrence Brings hastened to explain that his wife and son do get to see him at mealtime at least once a week. 'Saturday is the day I clean up around home. I'm home for lunch then.'"

The reporter also mentioned that Brings was an extremely busy businessman, directing the destinies of his two play-publishing houses in Minneapolis and Chicago. "Today he figures he is the largest publisher of amateur plays in the world, from the standpoint of sales volume and number of titles."

Always forging ahead—never standing still! In 1950, Lawrence Brings made a new move upward to the roomy 50,000 square feet of space on three floors of a commercial building on the fringe of the Minneapolis shopping district. Before he finished, he would occupy an address stretching from 309 to 321 Fifth Avenue South.

Through all those years, he had been doing business with the same printing company. Lawrence invited them to move their equipment into the first floor of the building.

The President of T. S. Denison and Northwestern Press must have discovered he had a couple of spare minutes in his hard-working days and nights, and he was not about to fritter them away. Seizing the opportunity to branch out in the publishing business, he and Keith founded The Brings Press, a quality printing firm that would handle everything from letterheads to high school and college yearbooks. The yearbooks were works of art and brought orders from major colleges, including the University of Chicago. St. John's University at Collegeville, Minnesota, took top national honors with a Brings Press annual.

It was only a short walk down the stairs from Lawrence's editorial offices to his "other world"— where linotypes clicked and presses thumped and rolled. He was in constant touch with printers and artists, and visitors would see him pause to study random press runs on his way to check a specific job. He could be alert to a dozen diversions along the way—and never forget his original objective.

Lawrence had been commuting back and forth to the T. S. Denison operation in Chicago, but a new pattern was beginning to emerge in 1950. It could have been appropriate to move the Brings interests to Chicago any time after the purchase of T. S. Denison in 1944.

Lawrence Brings does admit that he has made mistakes with investments. The most unfortunate investment was made when he was sales-pressured by a personal friend to buy vacant lots in a Chicago suburb on a monthly payment basis. He soon discovered that the real estate taxes began to soar to the point where it would be unwise to continue making payments. He allowed the lots to revert back to the county and stopped making more payments.

But his interest in the acquisition of land persisted and later he bought acreages in the Minneapolis area which he later sold at a tremendous profit. His son always said that he should have continued in the real estate business. His real estate profits made it possible to acquire a plant for the publishing business.

Leaving Minneapolis would have meant breaking his very unique ties with Central Lutheran Church, and one distinguished Minneapolitan was so alarmed at the prospect that he put his apprehensions into a 1950 New Year's letter to Larry Brings. Clifford C. Sommer, who was then an officer of Midland National Bank and a member of the Board of Trustees of Central Lutheran Church, began by expressing his personal appreciation and thanks to Lawrence ". . . for the many accomplishments that you have brought to our church . . . The fact that much of your efforts are unnoticed by the membership at large, because so much you do is in the background, tends in my mind to add worthiness to your efforts . . ."

Then Mr. Sommer got to the heart and soul of the matter: "In the past couple of weeks I have heard disquieting rumors that you have been thinking, a little at least, of transferring your residence to Chicago." He expressed "a fervent wish" that Lawrence Brings would remain in Minneapolis.

Beyond the expectation that Larry would miss his friends tremendously and be missed, Clifford Sommer emphasized the greater glory of his "mission" to Central Lutheran Church. Although others might aspire to the role of leadership, he felt that Larry was "the only person with the energy, ingenuity, time, judgment, patience, even temperament and confidence" to qualify for such a mighty challenge—"the renaissance of Central."

In wrapping up his New Year's message to the Brings family, Mr. Sommer expressed a wish that "all your thinking be blessed so that you will do what you feel necessary and desirable for your family and you." But it was obvious that he hoped the "blessed thinking" would lead the Brings family to continued attendance at Central Lutheran Church every Sunday—and to all the weekday meetings and services that might seem "rudderless" without the energetic presence of Lawrence M. Brings.

Aside from his talents as a bright and shining money-raiser for Central, Larry had formed many church friendships. He was not a "stuffy" Christian. His office phone often rang with fraternal as well as business calls. On one occasion, a listener heard him answer in this manner, "How are you? Oh! Well, that's what you get for drinking and carousing around!" From the grin on Larry's face, it was obvious the caller was a person of sober dignity and consequence.

With the acquisition of The Brings Press, it became unlikely that the business would be shifted to Chicago. In a couple of years, the printing company decided to sell their interest and equipment, and Lawrence bought the entire plant. Now he had everything he needed for publication purposes, in one building in a convenient location in Minneapolis. There was even a branch post office one block away, perfect for mailing out correspondence, promotion literature and shipments of books.

Early in the 1950s, Lawrence made up his mind to transfer T. S. Denison to Minneapolis and concentrate all his editorial and publishing activities at the headquarters on Fifth Avenue South. He moved the Denison inventory, but the office equipment was destined to remain in Chicago.

Mr. Eben Holmes Norris, whose demise enabled Larry to buy T. S. Denison, has already been described as a stickler for office efficiency. "He had that network of complicated filing systems in compartmentalized cabinets," Lawrence still recalls with awe. "Everything was indexed and cross-indexed and had to be filed exactly right. Well, do you know what? I sold that elaborate office equipment within six months for the same price I had paid for T. S. Denison. In other words, I got T. S. Denison for nothing!" he exclaimed triumphantly. Undoubtedly Lawrence Brings has a faculty for being at the right place at the right time, with just the right amount of money and nerve to be a fantastic horse-trader.

T. S. Denison was an internationally famous old firm, and its arrival in Minneapolis caused a stir in theatrical, educational and newspaper circles. After more than two decades, there are still a few people who think that T. S. Denison is Chicago-based. This story will set them straight.

Bob Murphy celebrated the occasion with a feature in the *Minneapolis Star,* saluting the new arrival with flamboyant rhetoric: "An unheard-of thunder begins to be noted throughout the land, and it's composed of the treading of boards and the mouthing of lines.

"A great deal of this board-treading and line-mouthing originates at a Minneapolis address, 309-21 Fifth Avenue S., new home of twin organizations, The Northwestern Press and T. S. Denison & Co."

Mr. Murphy noted that Denison and Northwestern plays would be responsible for some 20,000 productions that season, with an audience of some six million persons. The two companies would offer 6,000 to 7,000 play titles, which certainly made it a "big business." The Brings family tried to add a hundred new titles a year, while dropping about the same number.

The reporter turned his attention to the sources of all that brain-straining. "Authors in some cases are on a royalty basis, others are paid outright for their product," wrote Mr. Murphy. "Some of Northwestern and Denison's scripts call for royalties, as well as purchase of the scripts, others do not. In the case of musicals, it rents complete orchestrations."

There was this colorful note: "One author, Charles George, spends full time turning out musical comedies. Available are records of George singing correctly his own melodies. They can be rented or bought."

When the themes of successful plays became obsolete or unfashionable, they were sometimes revised. An anti-Nazi play could be fitted up with a Communist bogeyman, for instance. Some of the productions kept rolling off the press endlessly, completely intact. That was the case with Jay Tobias' "Here Comes Charlie," which had sold 250,000 copies between 1937 and 1953. Robert St. Clair had turned out so many "best sellers" that he was writing under four or five pseudonyms to avoid repetition in the catalog.

Amateur play-acting was at its sparkling peak in the early 1950s, with 350,000 customers on the Northwestern-Denison mailing list. Had movies and radio been a threat? On the contrary. Lawrence Brings even seemed optimistic about the "moving pictures" that were coming out of boxes in American living rooms. He believed the constant growth of amateur dramatics was due to the triple influences of radio, television and movies. People were seeing and hearing more acting, "and they were moved to go and do likewise."

There were no ominous warnings at that time, but it was typical of Lawrence Brings to broaden his base of operations. In addition to publishing books about play production and radio programming, he had started compiling a volume of television techniques. He had also acquired the American publishing rights to the English book, "Count Folke Bernadotte," by Ralph Hewins. As long as Larry had his own printing plant in the building, he certainly would make use of it.

Ethel was as much at home in the building on Fifth Avenue South as her husband and son. Lawrence often says of Ethel, "We were partners in every way!" When a new piece of processing equipment was installed, they would come back in the evening and learn to operate it. They were fascinated with inserting machines and presses, and it was a challenge to see whether they could "outdo the professionals" in speed and skill.

Lawrence and Ethel spent the finest hours of their personal lives at Knollwood for fourteen years. Their handsome home was an architectural jewel, in a setting of magnificently landscaped grounds. It was furnished and decorated with all the good taste that Ethel had never been able to lavish on the boardinghouse rooms and apartments that had been their earlier residences.

Ethel was a gracious, lively hostess. Her sense of humor was keenest when she entertained her friends and coworkers from the office. People remember that she was rather quiet and reserved, letting Larry hold the center of the stage, when they attended meetings and socials at Central Lutheran Church. Her regal poise and equanimity were most apparent at the T. S. Denison plant. When Ethel walked around the office with a sheaf of invoices or correspondence in her hand you knew she had to be a *somebody*. Strangers were not surprised to learn that she had been a concert violinist.

In spite of her great sense of humor, Ethel was a businesslike perfectionist. If anyone made an error around the office, she went straight to the source and demanded to know how it had happened and why. She was orderly and well-disciplined herself, and she expected other people to conduct themselves in the same manner.

Chapter Fourteen

This Is Your Life!

How many lives can one man live? As the 1950s rolled forward and people enjoyed staying at home in front of their television sets, the demand for amateur stage productions gradually decreased. T. S. Denison would continue to offer an adequate list of plays, but Lawrence Brings was already shifting into high gear as a book publisher.

Nothing in Life Is Free, by Della Gould Emmons, was one of his first ventures into a highly competitive new field. The story of Sacajawea, the Indian heroine of the Lewis and Clark expedition, was later made into a motion picture. Lawrence often used Mrs. Emmons as an example of a successful author. She was even invited to Hollywood as a consultant during the filming of her book.

Another popular title was *Living God's Way,* a book of devotions by Dr. Reuben K. Youngdahl, the distinguished Lutheran minister. On publication date in Minneapolis, most of Dr. Youngdahl's congregation lined up for autographed copies.

Soon the publisher became an author! Lawrence Brings had resisted the urge to be a playwright, but his background as a speech teacher inspired him to write *Clever Introductions for Chairmen*. Recognizing the demand for books of that type, he also wrote or compiled *The Master Guide for Speakers, Modern Book of Christmas Plays, Golden Book of Church Plays, Humorous Introductions for Emcees, The Master Pep Book, The Clubwoman's Entertainment Book* which features everything from plays and skits to pageants—and other practical program aids that have sold in the thousands over the years.

One of Lawrence Brings' finest achievements during the 1950s was *We Believe in Prayer*, a compilation of enlightening essays by President Dwight D. Eisenhower, Abba Eban, Wernher von Braun, Kate Smith, George Meany, and many other famous personalities in the modern world. Excerpts of *We Believe in Prayer* were printed in *Reader's Digest* and in nearly one hundred metropolitan newspapers as a daily Lenten series.

During an autographing session, two venerable old friends were waiting in line for copies of *We Believe in Prayer*. Lawrence looked up, thrilled and surprised to see the Rev. C. E. Benson who had opened his heart and home in Stillwater, almost forty years before, to a young subscription-solicitor who was determined to go to college. Poignant memories overflowed as Lawrence looked past the Rev. Benson's shoulder and saw the face of Herman Samuelson. Here was the former Executive Secretary to Gov. Eberhart—the judge at the 1915 Luther League Speech Contest who had bestowed kind words as well as first prize on a high school student named Larry Brings.

It was a sentimental moment when Lawrence M. Brings, publisher and author, wrote in both books: "In appreciation to you for helping a young boy go to college." When the Rev. C. E. Benson read the inscription in his copy of *We Believe in Prayer,* the tears poured down his cheeks. Two years later the Rev. Benson died, but their friendship would remain alive in the story of Lawrence's life.

We Believe in Prayer is typical of the "yardstick" that LMB uses in evaluating any manuscript. He asks himself, "Is this a novelty subject, good only for the moment? Will it be outdated in a couple of months?" If the answer is yes, the manuscript will be rejected. Lawrence Brings looks for books with enduring qualities that will continue to interest readers and historians, for one reason or another, for decades to come. Some of them might require updating or revising, but the general subject matter must not be "faddish."

Classroom materials and teachers' aids became some of T. S. Denison's most staple book items. LMB was delighted with the widespread demand for Mary Jackson Ellis' *Kindergarten Log* which was published in 1955. Subsequent grade school logs were written by Mrs. Ellis, with collaborators, and were extremely successful.

Lawrence Brings went into the book-publishing business with the same exuberance that had characterized his speech school and play-publishing activities. It was another upward crest, but books are unpredictable—and occasionally they did not live up to his high expectations.

How does a poor boy from a truck farm in Little Canada finally become a book publisher? Now we know. He faces the facts of life, but he does not allow them to conquer him—and he advises everyone else to do the same!

In addition to all that writing and publishing, Lawrence could enjoy reaping the fruits of an earlier endeavor—in satisfaction, if not in money. Wherever he turned, he learned that he had been responsible for the fluent preaching styles of hundreds of Lutheran pastors. They had heeded his advice: "Be natural and sincere, avoid a ministerial manner."

He had left his imprint on the careers of successful lawyers, businessmen, salesmen and teachers. One of his prize students is United States Federal Judge Edward J. Devitt. Another was Ed Peterson, a future president of the American Florists Association, who said, when he introduced him as the speaker at a Kiwanis meeting, "He was one of my professors at the 'U,' and his speech courses meant more than all the others in my self-development."

It is generally agreed that he forced them to confront their stage fright in his classes and taught them to overcome it. On one occasion, when he was in the elevator at the Athletic Club, a fellow-passenger looked at him twice and then asked, "Aren't you Lawrence Brings?"

Lawrence admitted that he was.

The other man told him, "I was in your public speaking class at the 'U,' and you scared the hell out of me—but you taught me to talk in public." He is now an attorney in Minneapolis. With rare modesty, Lawrence Brings always seems pleasantly surprised when he is given credit for his former students' eloquence.

It is difficult to keep track of LMB's philanthropic activities in the 1950s. We can only wonder how one man could have handled all of them. He was not just a "joiner." Whenever he became involved in anything, he worked to improve it—to give it additional zest and purpose. By 1953, he had been a member of the Board of Trustees of Central Lutheran Church for fourteen years and had been its Chairman for eleven years.

Lawrence had organized and was serving as President of the Central Lutheran Church Foundation — which had become a "sequel" to his bond-buying campaign after the Depression. He had just been elected President of the newly organized Minnesota Protestant Foundation. He was also active in the Minnesota Council of Churches, Minneapolis Hospital Research Council, and all those other organizations that were mentioned in an earlier chapter.

In 1954, the congregation of Central Lutheran Church knew that this man had earned special recognition. At a dinner meeting on April 23, Pastor Elmer S. Hjortland announced that the highlight of the evening would be a surprise performance called THIS IS YOUR LIFE, patterned after the well-known television program. A baby picture was flashed on the screen, and Pastor Hjortland explained with witty candor:

"It was on September 29, 1897, at 8 a.m. that Larry Brings first saw the light of day. This was the most significant event on that day, as diligent search of historical records shows no other world-shattering episode occurred. We couldn't even find a picture of the event, so we used the next best here—that of Keith. Isn't he cute?

"But to come back to Larry," Pastor Hjortland continued. "He was born in those '90s that witnessed the panic of '93 and the Spanish-American War. It was into the Cleveland-McKinley world that Larry came to make his way. He is a living example of the American way of life . . ."

Lawrence's mother, who would live to be eighty-three, was there to look back over the years of early hardship and think how far her oldest son had come —to be honored on this night in this great Minneapolis church! Did she realize that her own dauntless spirit had always throbbed within him, propelling him onward and upward since boyhood?

As THIS IS YOUR LIFE continued, there were recollections of Larry's confirmation at Arlington Hills Lutheran Church. Then Mrs. Flora Mutsch, his sister, recalled that Larry was a good student. She said, "In the 1916 Senior Annual of Central High, St. Paul, the quotation under his name states, 'You are an excellent scholar, having the graces of speech and skill in the turning of phrases.' Dramatics, debate and literary activities were Larry's interests."

Judge Luther W. Youngdahl was there to laud his fellow-Gustavian with this salute: "To Larry we owe a great debt of gratitude not only for his college leadership, but for his unique service in developing financial resources for the college through the Bernadotte Foundation." Judge and Mrs. Youngdahl came out from behind the curtain on the stage to congratulate Larry and Ethel "on the magnificent job that they have done for Central."

There was a review of Larry Brings' early teaching experiences at New Richmond, and Hugo A. Carlson revived his fond memories of Larry's and Ethel's wedding day.

Here again were words of appreciation for a former speech teacher. Pastor Hjortland noted that many pastors of the Evangelical Lutheran Church and the United Lutheran Church owed their platform delivery to their training under Professor Brings, and Pastor Robert G. Borgwardt seconded the motion: "We at Seminary recall particularly your emphasis on phonetics, movement of the lips— and the contortions you went through to get us to limber up."

Pastor Hjortland, who would serve as Senior Pastor from 1945 to 1955, had come to Central in time to appreciate Lawrence Brings' unswerving dedication to *undebtedness*. He spoke highly of Lawrence's "faith in the people of Central to rise out of their difficulties and to give a firm foundation to its financial affairs."

Clifford C. Sommer, who was on comfortable terms with large figures as a banker, was glad that Lawrence Brings had not moved to Chicago in 1950. He told a "fascinating story" about the way Larry had hacked away at the huge debt that shackled their beautiful new church after the Depression. In 1928, the total indebtedness was $659,328. By 1940, it was down to $541,300. The actual indebtedness on the night of THIS IS YOUR LIFE was down to $177,000, and Mr. Sommer looked forward to total liquidation of the entire debt by 1959. Turning his attention back to Lawrence Brings, Mr. Sommer announced, "It has been through your persistent efforts that the debt of Central Lutheran became a controlled debt."

Much of the history of Central Lutheran Church, it developed, was woven into the tapestry of Lawrence Brings' own life. Pastor Hjortland spoke of the establishment of the Endowment Fund and the organization of the Central Lutheran Foundation which grew from $66,000 in 1943 to $383,000 in 1953. It was a case of financial genius—paying off the debt with one hand and putting money into the bank with the other—to provide an astounding fiscal balance.

Laurence L. Lunden, vice-president of the University of Minnesota, pointing to a comparison chart, declared, "It was your idea, Larry, and some of us had to be sold on the idea. But we are sold now! While you worked at the reduction of the debt, you at the same time insisted on building the endowment fund. The result? By 1951 we could honestly say that we had control of our debt by having the majority of church bonds held in the endowment fund. The indebtedness (the red columns) kept shrinking and the endowment fund (the black columns) kept growing."

To reduce the picture to simpler terms, it was like putting money into a savings account while you are paying off the installments on your electric stove. If you work hard enough at it, you will end up owning the stove and still have money drawing interest in the bank—to help pay for the next appliance. Some people might say, "Why shouldn't we use that extra money to pay for the stove?" According to Lawrence Brings, you would be likely to fritter everything away and end up with no money in the bank at all.

The dreams for a "Greater Central" had persisted through the years, but the church leaders had learned caution during the Depression. As Pastor Hjortland noted, "For many years Central Lutheran needed a parish house and a memorial chapel. In those days in the '40s there did not seem to be much hope for a Greater Central. However, the dream persisted and today we are well on the way to the accomplishment of a goal which you have done much to achieve."

Lawrence Brings was personally sentimental about the latest 1954 achievement, which was described that night by P. Don Carson: "It was in the last days of 1951 that ground was broken for the first unit of the Sunday School Building—the beginning of Greater Central. At a total cost of $291,-000, it is now completely paid for in full, and we can feel confident in moving ahead to the next development of our building program."

In the production of THIS IS YOUR LIFE, Larry Brings was a popular character on pictures relating to Greater Central's building program, fishing on Lake Minnetonka, and having fun at a Rotarians' costume party dressed as a Chinaman.

Pastor Hjortland concluded the program of happy memories by telling the group, "This is the man whom we honor tonight and give our heartfelt thanks for his friendship and his service to Central Lutheran

Church." Pastor Hjortland then presented Lawrence Brings with a plaque which stated:

Central Lutheran Church
of
Minneapolis
Recognition Award
Presented to
Lawrence M. Brings
April 23, 1954

In appreciation of his 30 years of loyalty, devotion, and unselfish service to his church and to his God.

In his Press Proofs for April 1954, Larry writes from the *Editor's Desk:*

Dale Carnegie says, "A third of the people who rush to psychiatrists for help could probably cure themselves if they would get interested in helping others."

Some people think they can donate a few dollars to charity and then close the book. But if you really want to get interested in life, try to understand the problems of those around you —the postman, the delivery boy, the student working his way through college, your employees—yes, and your customers.

These people are human beings like us— they are bursting with troubles, dreams and ambitions like us. They need sympathy, advice, a brotherly hand; remember it doesn't cost any time to smile.

But if you really want to make an investment that pays big dividends—put a few hours a week into the Boy Scouts, your Sunday School or some other antidote for juvenile delinquency.

Don't try to thumb a ride through life and cry if you miss the big parade. This is the season of Spring planting; try to plant a few kind words every day and watch the flowers of joy come up.

That was a thrilling night for Lawrence Brings, who had given so much of his life—so enthusiastically—to Central Lutheran. When he had joined the church, Dr. Stub was the only pastor. On the night of THIS IS YOUR LIFE in 1954, there were five pastors carrying on the spiritual work at Central.

Looking around him, Lawrence could feel the warm fellowship of lifetime friends. Many of them autographed his copy of the evening's script.

There were many admirers—dear hearts and gentle people—who could only be with Lawrence in spirit on the night of THIS IS YOUR LIFE. He still cherishes this telegram that a young nephew and his wife sent from New Haven:

We are thinking of you tonight and wish that we might be there to join with the congregation and friends in honoring you. As it is, we must send our congratulations from New Haven. Central Lutheran, ministering to the needs of its people in Minneapolis, will long remain a living testimony to your organizational efforts and persistent moral stamina to uphold the church in times of need. Carol and I rejoice with you for the many blessings of life which you have freely received and freely given in the service of others. Good luck, Uncle Lawrence, and again, congratulations. CAROL AND ROGER.

Roger Johnson, Lawrence's nephew, has been head of the department of religion at Wellesley College for the past fifteen years.

In May 1954, the *Greater Minneapolis* Magazine, a Chamber of Commerce publication, turned its editorial searchlight on the "Foundation Man" and his extraordinary hobby. Lawrence Brings was pictured at the top of the page, examining architects' plans for the Greater Central building program which was largely financed by the Foundation.

"Hobbies are usually thought of as avocations which improve the mind and spirit but which are unrewarding financially," the reporter wrote. "It is therefore unusual to find a Minneapolis man who has a hobby which not only gives him respite from his workaday affairs, but also is profitable—to others.

"Devotee of this unusual pastime is Lawrence M. Brings, president of T. S. Denison & Co. and The Brings Press. Brings, who is known to his friends as Larry, spends his spare time starting worthwhile foundations."

The history of the Central Lutheran Foundation was reviewed. Larry spoke of its goals and lofty expectations—"to receive gifts, hold the principal of such gifts in perpetuity and to expend the income therefrom for educational, charitable and religious purposes . . ." Most of the original sponsors expected the Foundation funds to reach about $50,000—instead of "a whopping $384,000" by 1954 and still climbing! Knowing Lawrence Brings, we might guess the sky would be the limit in laying up provisions for the future in this "heavenly treasury."

Larry told of his countless visits to church members—of explaining the fund to them and describing the good works that it could accomplish. "I found I had to polish my sales talk," he recalled. "People are usually frugal and often they fear that the money for which they have worked hard will be spent foolishly. We found that the device of holding the principal in perpetuity allayed their fears—in this way only the income from the donations could be used and the original amount remained intact."

The Foundation had underwritten the construction of the $287,000 Central Sunday School Building, and it would do the same for the purchase of parking space. The loans were being repaid on a monthly basis by the congregation. Here was a church that could borrow from itself!

After Lawrence Brings proceeded to set up the Minnesota Protestant Foundation as his third spiritual enrichment enterprise, his fame spread far and wide. Most churches were in the habit of barely skimming along the sharp limits of their building programs, interest payments, and annual expenses. How could this layman do such a gigantic job of "laying up treasures on earth" for Central Lutheran Church, when so many pastors had to entreat their congregations, Sunday after Sunday, to be more generous? What was his singular approach? If it worked for him, why couldn't it work for other churches, church schools and religious organizations?

They soon learned that he was not stingy with advice. Although Lutheran groups were the first to consult him, he has been glad to instruct other denominations in the fine art of setting up foundations. He has always been in favor of individuals and institutions putting away some reserve funds—as a cushion against adversities over which they might have no control.

Chapter Fifteen

Through an Author's Eye

Dynamic book salesman, protector of defenseless authors, editorial superman, or guardian of the royalties? How does a publisher look to one of his authors?

Lawrence Brings' wavy brown hair was receding toward the back of his head when I first met him in 1955. Judging from earlier pictures of him, he had gained some weight since his college and speech-teaching days—but he still had a puckish smile, even when he was concentrating on business.

Truly Latchaw, who had written a play for T. S. Denison, invited me to go with her when she visited the publishing company. Little did I realize how familiar those offices would become in future years!

When Truly introduced me to Lawrence Brings as the author of a recently published novel which I had dedicated to her, he expressed an eagerness to read it. At that time I did not know of his lifelong interest in religious scholarship and literature, but I appreciated his inquiries about *The Rock and the Sand.*

It was more than a matter of politeness. On April 12, 1955, he wrote: "I have finished the reading of the book and I was impressed with your treatment. Your phrasing caught the spirit of the period and you sustained interest in a moving plot until the very end . . . My only regret is that I didn't get the manuscript to examine before your present publisher did."

That was the beginning of a long-time association with Lawrence Brings. When he heard I was completing another biblical novel, he asked to see the manuscript. Two months later, when LMB sent me a contract covering the publication of *Search for Eden* by T. S. Denison, he wrote, "I hope we will both be satisfied with this venture and that our faith in this book will be justified by the final results. . . I hope, too, that this venture will start off a period of pleasant association. I expect that you will continue writing and that we may publish your creations." We started off with high hopes, and sixteen years later my Denison "creations" numbered fourteen.

In the promotion for *Search for Eden* back in 1956, Mr. Brings stressed that we should emphasize the main theme — "man's continuous search for Eden." Characteristically, he was disturbed about some amorous passages that would be considered very mild in the 1970s. A slight confrontation developed across the paper-strewn desk in his office. He was thinking of the sensitivity of his "special public" when he asked me to tone down some of the "sex references."

The reactions of several book dealers were sought, and I even took the controversial material to my parish priest who said we could not close our eyes to the fact that there is sin in the world—which is the reason why the Ten Commandments are necessary.

Most of the "search for sex" stayed in the book, along with the "search for Eden," and I am probably the only T. S. Denison author who can make that claim. Somehow, it doesn't seem that important in retrospect. Sex has become overrated, degraded, and commercialized in pornographic bookstores. The old literary finesse has been replaced by a cheap product, peddled with slobbering tediousness. Ho-hum.

Search for Eden, in keeping with the Noah theme, received a deluge of reviews, most of them extremely favorable. It was also published in the United Kingdom. Soon Mr. Brings acquired the rights to *The Rock and the Sand,* which had gone into a Belgian edition by that time. Some of the reviewers suggested that both of those books could be filmed as motion picture "spectaculars," and Lawrence and I still agree with them—even though it may happen posthumously for both of us.

After discussing my next theme with Lawrence Brings, I started writing *Son of Nazareth*—a fictional story of Jesus during the "hidden years" of His life. In case I didn't already feel reverent enough, LMB cautioned, ". . . it is very important that there be no sexy treatment in the story. It would be out of key with the general theme." True. Let Kazantzakis do it—this would not be another *Last Temptation of Christ.*

Christmas was coming, but my royalties were only dribbling in. I asked for an advance, and Lawrence Brings sent it—with this observation: "Here it is! And, you'll be sorry in January that you spent it when the next report comes along." I was becoming accustomed to LMB's witticisms about money.

During a discussion about promotion during those early years, I mentioned that many of the best-selling authors were noted for their eccentricities. "Maybe I should do something spectacular?" I suggested.

"That's a great idea!" he said. "Why don't you walk around the top of the Foshay Tower, without holding on?" At that time the Foshay Tower was the tallest skyscraper in Minneapolis.

There were some mild disagreements about punctuation during my first years as a T. S. Denison author. On one occasion, LMB wrote: "As I have checked over the manuscript, I come up against the problem of hyphenating. It has always been my belief that a hyphen is to be used in certain words to split two vowels. What is your understanding of this rule? Perhaps you can have an answer when you come in.

"I notice, too, that in your style of construction you use frequently the semicolon with a continuation of the thought without starting a new sentence. What is your policy on this?"

It was obvious that he preferred crisp sentences, with as few conjunctions as possible. This was his editorial prerogative, and I was expected to justify my convoluted rhetoric.

We had a hassle about commas, too—at a time when they were being considered unfashionable. He maintained that the elimination of commas permitted faster reading. I maintained that readers might become lost in a comma-less sentence, especially when the dependent clause preceded the independent clause—and have to waste time backtracking. There is more to writing books than just putting words on paper. Editorial conferences can also be spirited.

The Minneapolis publisher still found time to make some speeches during those years. Often he talked about the fine art of public speaking, using his own speech books as points of reference and enlightenment—with humor and super-salesmanship. Sometimes he received complimentary letters about his speeches, with inquiries about stores where his books could be purchased.

On one memorable occasion, Lawrence Brings' extemporaneous speech talents extricated this author from a nightmare situation. Neophyte authors are inclined to suffer from stage-fright, and I had never taken one of Professor Brings' speech courses. After my second biblical novel was published, both my publisher and I were invited to a luncheon in honor of the event. I was scheduled to be the main speaker before an audience of book dealers, librarians, authors and various local dignitaries.

I had prepared my speech carefully, with notes, explaining the source of inspiration for the book, how I developed the plot from a few sparse sentences in Genesis, and some of my research and personal experiences. I knew what I was going to say.

It would have been far, far better if I had arrived late. During the five minutes before the luncheon, I had a cozy chat with the master of ceremonies who was going to introduce me. He asked question after question with sincere interest and sympathy. Evidently I told him *all*.

With the luncheon eaten, the charming young master of ceremonies arose to his feet to introduce me. I sat there—horrified and petrified—listening to him deliver my entire speech, point by point.

After an eternity I heard my name announced and tottered reluctantly to my feet, darting desperate glances at my notes and realizing they had been stripped bare. Somehow I pulled a few minor observations out of the air and read several paragraphs from the introduction to the book—which the master of ceremonies did not yet have a copy of.

I cast an apprehensive glance at Lawrence Brings who was sitting calmly beside me—except that I was standing up. Did he understand my agony? "Perhaps my publisher would like to add a few words," I stuttered.

He stood up, and I collapsed. He talked at length about his first meeting with me, his interest in religious themes, and his faith in that new book. I thanked heaven for a publisher who could rescue me from the most "speech-less" fiasco of my life! Since that time, I am pretty cagey about confiding in masters of ceremony. I won't even give them my social security number until after I have finished talking!

When it is a family business, an author becomes aware of the other people who are closely associated with her publisher. I first heard of Ethel Brings when her husband said with a chuckle, "My wife just finished reading your *Search for Eden* manuscript. She doesn't believe anyone in Minnesota could have written it!" I appreciated the compliment and paid special attention to the lady when I met her.

Ethel was often in the large outer office consulting with the secretaries and order clerks, while Keith kept an eye on business all over the plant. It was exciting to walk up the stairs and into the office, with its display of T. S. Denison books in a long glass showcase.

Lawrence Brings had a large, paneled personal office, and it was often piled high with material that was awaiting his attention. Unlike Eben Holmes Norris, the office efficiency expert in Chicago, LMB did not choose to waste valuable time and space with fancy filing systems. His small filing cabinet bulged, and his desk and chairs were piled high with correspondence, manuscripts, and assorted books and papers. But Larry Brings had everything under control. He had a well-organized mind—a mental filing system equipped with a photographic memory. Occasionally he would look at his crowded office and say there wasn't enough space for all his business, but he knew where everything was.

In 1955, Lawrence and Ethel sold their lovely Park Terrace home at Knollwood and moved to an apartment at 2615 Park Avenue in Minneapolis, but they continued to spend their summers at Lake Minnetonka.

Later they decided to build a new home at Lake Minnetonka, and they made frequent trips there during its construction. They were looking forward to that exciting new phase in their lives when they learned that Ethel had developed cancer. Surgery followed and treatment was begun. Ethel and Lawrence hoped, for four years, that the condition could be held in check. They had faced so many crises and triumphed over them. Here was the greatest challenge of them all.

Ethel continued to spend some time in the office, giving personal attention to orders and business correspondence. The tall lady, with her confident personality, still seemed to dominate the office at T. S. Denison—even when she was receiving cobalt treatments.

After it became apparent to Ethel that her illness was terminal, Lawrence remembers that she was sometimes overwhelmed with hopelessness when she was alone with him. On their trips to inspect the new house under construction at the lake, she would say, "What a beautiful place! But I'll never live in it."

Her heartsick husband would try to cheer her up by answering, "Of course you will," and making jokes that sometimes taxed his eloquence beyond endurance.

During the last two years of Ethel's illness, she often awoke groaning with pain in the night. After awhile, she needed medication every two hours, and her husband felt that he should be the one to take care of her.

Lawrence Brings had a conference with his son. He told Keith that he wanted to devote his entire time, day and night, to minister to his desperately sick wife. Keith, he said, could do his share by taking full responsibility for running the business. Thus, they divided their burdens during that trying period.

Ethel was able to live in the new house at the lake for six weeks. There, at Christmas time, she sat erect in a chair—a lady of gallant fortitude—looking outwardly joyful and pleased with the antics of her grandchildren and the family festivities.

When Ethel passed away on March 10, 1960, Lawrence looked back over the thirty-nine years of their married life and business partnership. "We worked so hard during those early years," he recalls, more with appreciation than regret.

The funeral at Central Lutheran Church was attended by some of the most distinguished citizens of Minneapolis who had known Ethel and Larry Brings through the years. Much to the amazement of the bereaved husband, there was a visitor from Chicago at the funeral—the man who had vowed many years ago that he would never marry anyone if Ethel would not be his wife. He had remained a bachelor.

Ethel had received a partner's share of the business profits, and she and Lawrence had set up separate trust funds. Ethel's money still remains in trust for her son. Lawrence says he bought insurance, too—when his family responsibilities increased—but, "I've never had much luck with the stock market. So I established trust funds at my bank."

It was natural that Ethel's death would signal the end of an era for Lawrence Brings. Feeling drained of emotion after that lengthy period of heartache and tension, he threw himself back into his work at T. S. Denison.

Over the years, he had often spoken of turning the responsibility for the company over to Keith. During those last years of the 1950s, Keith had more than his share of carrying the load—and T. S. Denison survived in fine shape.

Keith had his lovely wife, Barbara, and his attractive children to fill his life. When they were expecting their first baby, they had started looking for a house because children were not allowed in their apartment building. They found a house near Knollwood, quite near the elder Brings' home. Later Keith and his young wife built a home at Charleston Acres near Wayzata. They had financed all their own housing projects.

Both Keith and Barbara worried because Lawrence seemed "lost and alone" after Ethel's death. The elder Brings would not anticipate living alone in that beautiful new house at Lake Minnetonka. Before it was ever finished, it was crowded with sad memories for him.

Even as one partner took her last curtain call and departed from the scene, new Denison books were being born. Heading the list at that point was *Minnesota Heritage*, a large, handsome volume saluting Minnesota's first century of statehood. Before the Centennial in 1958, Truly Trousdale Latchaw started contacting scholars and leaders in all areas of Minnesota history — anthropology, education, religion, business, agriculture, politics, and the arts. Each contributor was an authority in his particular field.

The lavishly illustrated book, bound in rippled gold, lists Lawrence Brings as Editor-in-Chief, Truly Latchaw as Research Editor, and Edward Olderen and Howard Lindberg as Art Design Editors. Published in 1960, *Minnesota Heritage* is Lawrence Brings' idea of a perfect book. It will never be outdated as an enthralling source of information, enlightenment, and sheer reading enjoyment.

Chapter Sixteen

"Men of Achievement" Biographies

As a future biographer, it was fortunate that my family moved from White Bear Lake, Minnesota, to Winchester, Virginia, in the early 1960s. Otherwise, I would not have a treasure-trove of Lawrence Brings' letters in my files for present reference. The new location also enabled me to be within easy driving distance of the Library of Congress and distinguished sources of information in Washington, D. C.

By that time, T. S. Denison was publishing more than one new title a week in the juvenile, educational, fictional and religious fields. Lawrence and Keith Brings had discussed the wisdom of launching a special series of books—with "book club" possibilities.

In the spring of 1962, Lawrence sent me a handwritten letter that changed the course of my writing life. He had been in the hospital for three weeks and was recovering from a gall bladder operation—but that did not keep him from catching up on his correspondence. The subject of that letter was the "Men of Achievement" series.

My mind slipped back to 1957 when I had seen Mildred Comfort, one of our most prolific Minnesota authors, sitting in the St. Paul Public Library gathering material for a biography about J. Edgar Hoover. Mr. Brings noted that she had followed the same pattern with biographies about John Foster Dulles and Herbert Hoover. The design for a series had been established.

"The aim of these books is to show teen-agers the elements that make for success—a Horatio Alger type—the poor boy makes good," Mr. Brings wrote. In addition to a biography about 3M's William L. McKnight, which Mildred Comfort was completing, various authors were assembling the life stories of J. C. Penney, Lowell Thomas, Dr. Albert Schweitzer, and other appropriate prospects for the new T. S. Denison "Men of Achievement" series.

Lawrence Brings was concerned with developing variety—in biographical subjects and in authors' points of view. "Would you be interested in taking on an assignment to do one of these biographies?" he wrote. "I have Charles Kettering unassigned with a batch of source material furnished us." He suggested the names of several other prospects, and concluded, "Let me know what your reactions are to this proposal."

I had been bogged down in a long historical novel for several years, and I had always thought of myself as a fiction writer. Still, it might be a refreshing change of pace to see if I could write a biography. I chose Charles Kettering and went to work.

By the end of March, Lawrence Brings was healthy enough to use the typewriter again. He was glad I was willing to tackle the Kettering story.

I had considered the Kettering biography a one-shot assignment, but I soon caught the spirit of the man's tremendous imagination and hilarious sense of humor. Lawrence Brings was testing my talents as a biographer by asking to see the early chapters, but he soon told me to go ahead and finish writing the book.

In the meantime, back in Minnesota, Lawrence Brings was no longer feeling "lost and alone." Keith and Barbara had introduced him to Nettie Johnson, the widowed mother of one of their close friends, Patty. The vivacious Nettie was perfect for Lawrence Brings. After a short acquaintance, they were married January 9, 1961, with the enthusiastic approval of the young people on both sides of the family.

With Nettie and the "Men of Achievement" series to arouse his enthusiasm, Lawrence Brings' life took new directions. He and Nettie flew around the world for seven weeks in 1961 on a honeymoon trip.

Combined with the honeymoon were appointments with government officials in countries they were to visit, especially in Turkey, India, Thailand and Japan. Elmer L. Anderson, then governor of Minnesota, issued a special official document: "Be it known that L. M. Brings is hereby declared an ambassador of good will for the State of Minnesota, entitled to extend on behalf of the citizens in the state of Minnesota, all good wishes and due regard to the sovereign nations wherein he may travel." It opened the doors to important personages, among which was Prince Donay, the uncle of the King of Thailand, the chairman of his Privy Council. Both Lawrence and Nettie were guests in his home.

In 1962, when I was digging into the Kettering book, he wrote: "I am leaving Wednesday with my wife for the Seattle World's Fair and the Rotary Convention in Los Angeles . . . I move more slowly these days and I am sandwiching in vacation time. On June 20 we take a seven-days' cruise on the Great Lakes from Duluth to Buffalo and back. I'll be 65 in September and I plan to travel while I can navigate without crutches." After the lengthy period of tragedy and his major operation, he wanted to live his life to the fullest.

Lawrence Brings does not have a hypochondriac personality. He will mention that he has had periods of illness in his life, but he refuses to fret about them. That only aggravates the condition, he says. "I've learned to take the good and bad as they come," he often maintains, "because you can't change anything by worrying whether you'll survive for another week or another year. I live day by day by the grace of God."

In addition to taking care of my house and family, I was burning the midnight oil on the Kettering book. Lawrence Brings wrote in July that he hoped to have both the Kettering and J. C. Penney books listed in the new brochure by the fall of 1962. Mildred Comfort was looking forward to writing about Lowell Thomas—with an added thrill. "Mr. Thomas has invited her to spend a week or so in his home in

Pauling, New York, as his guest . . . She is quite excited about this invitation," LMB wrote.

After I mailed the completed Kettering manuscript to Lawrence Brings, I held my breath. On August 1, he sent some very complimentary remarks: "You have done a superb job on this biography and I feel that you were captivated by the subject himself . . . Congratulations on a good job! I don't want you to take a vacation, so get started on Sandberg."

He had mentioned that there might be other assignments, but I had been too busy to take them seriously. There was always the possibility that the Kettering book might not be acceptable. Now he wanted me to write about Carl Sandburg—a "dream assignment!" He had even arranged for me to interview the "Poet of the People" at Connemara Farm in Flat Rock, North Carolina.

This was heady fare for a novelist who had not known, at the beginning of that year, that she could teach herself to research and write a biography. It was work, but it was the kind of work I loved— tracking down information, checking dates and places, interviewing people, and capturing the whole picture between the pages of a "Man of Achievement" book. Before I had ever considered such a possibility, Mr. Brings' intuition had told him I could do it.

While I was concentrating furiously on Carl Sandburg at the Library of Congress, LMB kept mentioning future biographical prospects. In his letters he would say, "I don't want to overload you with assignments, but . . ." Additional authors were working industriously to build up the series which would eventually include Presidents Dwight D. Eisenhower, Lyndon B. Johnson and Richard M. Nixon—all of whom had started with "humble beginnings" and worked their way upward to the highest office in the land.

Sometimes we were swamped with more material than we could use in one medium-sized biography. On the subject of editing, Lawrence Brings often told his authors to "use their own judgment." If we did too much "editorializing," we had to justify it—with logic.

We were getting variety into the series, from J. Edgar Hoover and John Foster Dulles to Lowell Thomas, Carl Sandburg and Earnest Hemingway. Lawrence Brings revealed his "mental elasticity"— as opposed to the "intellectual arrogance" that was becoming so fashionable in publishing circles in the 1960s.

It was assumed that the "Men of Achievement" books would set young people a good example and stimulate them to make worthwhile use of their own talents. Many adults also considered them entertaining and inspiring. We were not "writing down" to anybody.

On that subject, Lawrence Brings declared, "It is true that all the books in the series will have general appeal regardless of the age of the reader."

That's the way it worked out. Over the years, I have received inquiries and comments from adults, as well as from students who were writing term papers about Carl Sandburg and my other biographical subjects. A lady inventor even wrote to me about my Charles Kettering biography.

The galleys of the Kettering book had been read and returned to Minneapolis by October 1, 1962. Larry Brings was "glad to hear that the interview with Carl Sandburg went well." My fascination must have been obvious, because LMB noted, "I can see you are enthusiastic about the Carl Sandburg assignment." There was some discussion about obtaining an appropriate picture for the cover—a game of "search and suspense" in some instances.

Those were years of hectic deadlines, with Lawrence Brings sometimes giving us overlapping assignments. I managed not to get the personalities of Carl Sandburg, Nathaniel Leverone, Harry Bullis and Carlos Romulo jumbled together. All great men leave "footprints in the sands of time," but they are as different and distinctive as fingerprints.

The publisher of the new series kept encouraging me to work and write harder, even when my back ached from long hours at the typewriter. He spurred me on with comments of this type: "It will be wonderful if you can finish the Sandburg book in time for the new brochure," and, "It's quite fantastic that you have been able to get along so well on the Leverone story. Good luck!'"

Even on research trips I had to keep my wits alert, but the sensation was "out of this world." The "Men of Achievement" books turned out to be flying carpets with jet motors for me.

It started with a plane trip to Palm Beach, Florida, to interview Nathaniel Leverone, the founder of the Canteen Company. Two months later I was invited back to Minneapolis in my old home state of Minnesota to research the scrapbooks of Harry Bul-

lis, the former President and Chairman of the Board
of General Mills.

When Harry and Mary Bullis invited Mr. and
Mrs. Brings and me to dinner at their handsome
Wayzata home, it was a special pleasure to meet
Nettie Brings for the first time. Nettie is the kind of
lady whom everybody loves immediately—completely compatible at first sight. Slim, attractive and
charming, she laughs easily and often.

As we were sipping cocktails, Nettie mentioned
that Mr. and Mrs. Leverone had taken them to The
Everglades for lunch when they were in Palm Beach
—a pleasure that I had enjoyed on my earlier visit.
"We made the mistake of ordering cocktails, without realizing that Mr. Leverone disapproved of drinking and smoking," Nettie said.

"I could have tipped you off," I said. "I had already run across that information in my research!"

"It turned out all right," Nettie chuckled. "As
soon as Mr. Leverone heard that my older son was a
graduate of Dartmouth, everything was forgiven.
We were buddy-buddies!" Nathaniel Leverone, as
one of Dartmouth's most loyal graduates, commissioned Pier Luigi Nervi to design the gigantic Field
House which stands as an architectural monument
to Mr. Leverone's memory at Dartmouth. These are
things we learn when we write biographies.

In February 1963, I wrote Lawrence Brings
about an illness in my family. He philosophized,
"You are in the doldrums now but usually there is
sunshine after the clouds." The next month he told
me not to take on any other assignments, because
he would be keeping me busy with future Men of

Achievement books. He wasn't making me rich, but he certainly was keeping me busy!

During that year, Larry Brings often sent good news about the series. For instance, "Just this morning I received a letter from the public relations director of the Penney Company that they plan to buy 2,000 copies of the book to distribute to the libraries of their various stores." Nathaniel Leverone had also ordered a special leather-bound edition of his biography.

Toward the end of 1963, it was my turn to have an operation. LMB wrote: "I hope that you come through your operation satisfactorily. Keep me advised of developments." In the same letter, he wanted to know whether I would write the Romulo biography. I couldn't even have my operation in peace! That was the way he approached the business of life, and he expected it to be contagious. Actually, it was.

The biography about General Carlos P. Romulo was one of the most thrilling experiences of my life, with two interviews with General Romulo in Washington and a meeting with him and his family of truly beautiful people—quite a few years later—in Manila.

The Bullis biography was on the press and the Romulo manuscript was completed when I realized my first "impossible dream"—to fly across the Atlantic to England for three weeks in the fall of 1964. After commenting that I had done "a good job" with the Romulo story, LMB added some typical remarks:

"You are a brave woman to venture alone on such an interesting trip. I'm afraid that you will have wished to stay longer when you get over there.

You will have a great deal to see . . . When I concluded a book deal with another author, she made a
trip home to England to visit her sister. It runs in
the air with you authors to spend your money as
soon as you receive it."

I laughed and laughed—and went flitting off to
London for my "vacation of a lifetime." The pleasures of that trip included a book fair in the Hay-
market and a visit to my British publishers' headquarters in Surrey.

The T. S. Denison presses were running at full
speed by December of that year. Lawrence Brings
was waiting for me to correct and return the Romulo
galleys when he wrote almost breathlessly, "I'm
very busy now and don't know how I can get out of
running around in circles. There are many things
that I must neglect."

I was busy, too, starting a biography about Hubert H. Humphrey, and packing for a trip to the
annual Penny Parade at the Carl Sandburg Birth-
place in Galesburg, Illinois.

It was Lawrence Brings who chose the subtitle for
the Humphrey book: *Champion of Human Rights.*
Whether they are DFLers or Republicans, Minne-
sotans feel a special warmth for Senator Humphrey
and want to give him all the credit he so richly
deserves.

Next came a biography about Melvin J. Maas—
one of Larry Brings' debating partners at old Central High in St. Paul—who became a Marine Corps
General, a Congressman from Minnesota, and the
Chairman of the President's Committee on Employment of the Handicapped after he lost his eyesight.

The inspirational "spin-off" on that assignment was tremendous. In the process, I met the delightful Maas family and many of Mel Maas' associates, shook the hand of President Lyndon B. Johnson, shook the "hook" of Harold Russell, called Senator "Mike" Mansfield off the Senate floor for a short interview, and talked with Commandant Wallace M. Greene Jr. at Marine Headquarters. There were several lively reunions with my dear friend, Grace Tully, the late President Roosevelt's secretary and author of *F.D.R., My Boss*.

A biographer is not expected to agree entirely with each man of achievement, but some sense of identification and enthusiasm are necessary ingredients. Lawrence Brings was always anxious to know whether we felt thrilled or excited about the accomplishments of our biographical subjects. If an author feels indifferent, he well knew, there is no zippy flavor of suspense or inspiration to pass on to the reader. That was the reason he usually wanted his authors to choose their own "Men of Achievement."

On May 29, 1965, at commencement, Lawrence Brings was awarded the alumni citation for "Distinguished Service and Significant Attainment in the Field of Business, and through this citation recognizes the added luster brought to the name of Gustavus Adolphus College by such service."

Larry and Nettie Brings had begun spending the frigid months at their winter home in Venice, Florida. In mid-February 1966, Lawrence made some comments about good reactions to the Humphrey and Maas biographies. As an authority on Minnesota weather, he wrote, "We expect to start driving back to Minneapolis the morning of the 25th and hope that we don't run into a snowstorm or blizzard."

The following June, he noted that inflation was catching up with the publishing business. He was regretfully raising the price of the "Men of Achievement" books as well as other Denison books. I was still working on the Maas manuscript, but a name in the Humphrey book had "rung a bell" in LMB's mind. I had mentioned that Hubert Humphrey's generation had grown up dancing to the music of Lawrence Welk in South Dakota. Since that included me, Larry Brings got in touch with "The Champagne Music Man." There are chain reactions everywhere, even in the publishing business. Lawrence Welk was scheduled to be my next "Man of Achievement."

Larry had taken a proud, fatherly interest in Nettie's family. He wrote in that June letter, "Nettie and I were down in Tucson, Arizona, the past week. Her son graduated from the University 'with distinction' and was commissioned a second lieutenant in the Army on the same day . . . Nettie's older son has declared himself as a candidate for the U. S. Senate in New Hampshire."

There was some earthshaking news in the fall of 1966. "I will have a tough season ahead of me since we have sold our property at 315 Fifth Avenue South and if we are able to get financing we plan to build a new plant in Bloomington," LMB wrote.

Waves of nostalgia swept over me as I remembered those old familiar upstairs offices and the printing and art departments on the first floor, outgrown for years but still dear to the hearts of T. S. Denison authors.

Build a new plant? I tried to visualize it. Undoubtedly Lawrence Brings was aiming toward another lofty crest—on the eve of his sixty-ninth birthday! He had delegated much of the executive authority to Keith, but his own hand was usually on the throttle in making major decisions.

In September he wrote of the Maas manuscript, "You have done a remarkably fine writing job and I am very pleased with it." Before the month was over, he sent me a check for my plane fare to Los Angeles—and I went flying off to interview Lawrence Welk and his "Music Makers" for ten days.

In the meantime, Lawrence Brings was proceeding with the building of a handsome new plant in suburban Bloomington. The pressses were still thumping so energetically—it almost sounded as though some T. S. Denison books might be published en route.

Before I had finished the Welk biography, I took off on a flying trip around the world—the most educational experience of my life, because it even included four days in Saigon. Larry Brings enjoyed my comments about the contrasting cultures and my impressions of the people in faraway places.

It was an advantage to have a mental picture of the Chinese faces in Saigon, Singapore and Bangkok when I wrote about Henry R. Luce who was born in China and spent his early life there. Later, when I wrote about another great world-traveler, Carl T. Rowan, I was glad I could visualize the foreign scenery that he describes so eloquently in his books, columns and articles.

On September 22, 1967, Lawrence Brings wrote that "We are now located in our new plant and have the task for the next two or three months of getting everything in place." During the move from the old plant, there was a period of panic when the pictures for the Lawrence Welk book were mislaid.

Lawrence Brings described the publication of the Lawrence Welk biography as "a long process" because of its size. "With 400 pages, the various forms will require two weeks just to print. Then will come the folding of the sheets, gathering the forms and sewing them, followed by the actual binding."

Sometimes LMB sounded depressed. Perhaps he had chosen an unfavorable time to invest in a large new publishing plant, with the handicaps of inflation, high printing costs, and cuts in school and library funds. Schools were often using copying machines, instead of buying books. In a couple of his 1968 letters he wrote, "It's been tough to carry the load of the new plant and the moving expenses involved," and, "We are having our problems of finance with the new building as well as with production."

Lawrence Brings sometimes mentioned cutting down on production, but he also wrote in one of those letters, "Keep on with the Luce book. When you finish it, I'll no doubt have another subject for you."

The teachers' aids and other educational materials continued to do well, but the "Men of Achievement" series did not always live up to its publisher's expectations. Had the 1960s been the wrong time in American history to glorify the "rags to riches" theme? Hippies seemed to enjoy wearing rags and sneering at the riches of "capitalist pigs." It is very possible that the pendulum will swing in the other direction, with maturity and more respect for the comforts of life. To be really chic in the literary-journalistic society of the 1960s, LMB should have published a series called "Hippie Hooligans." However, such ambiguous "heroes" would be too quickly outdated—there is nothing more pathetic than an old hippie.

Starting with only a handful of biographies in 1960, the "Men of Achievement" list now numbers more than fifty titles.

Chapter Seventeen

Inside the T. S. Denison Company

Lawrence Brings was trying to be more careful with his health, after a slight stroke in November, 1969. He later also developed a back condition and was wearing a back brace and trying to lose weight. Instead of dwelling on his miseries, he wrote almost jokingly, "Oh, well, I guess it's age creeping up on me and I must accept it. At least Nettie is in good health and she can take care of me." His hours at the office were supposed to be restricted, which meant that he probably went home a few minutes early.

Larry often made whimsical remarks about Nettie's sparkling good health. "She'll be able to push me around in my wheelchair!" he would say. From the way he was still rushing around at the age of seventy-five, Nettie would need to be a very fast sprinter with that wheelchair.

Shortly after we were settled in our new home in St. Paul, I went over to visit the new T. S. Denison Company building. Lawrence Brings gave me a grand tour of the handsome, spacious plant. It is all on one floor and spread over a large acreage, with convenient loading docks and parking areas. Under one roof are T. S. Denison and its four affiliates; The Northwestern Press, Denison Music Company, Handy Folio Music Company, and SELSCO.

The large reception room at the main entrance is bright and inviting. There are attractive displays of Denison books, and the grandfather clock from the old office stands in a position of honor.

All the departments are roomy, efficiently arranged, well-lighted and air-conditioned—with the presses, typesetting machines, and other printing equipment in a separate section on the west side of the building. Adjacent to the large mailing and order room, there is a huge warehouse department. In addition to T. S. Denison publications and novelties, I learned that books from the University of Minnesota Press are also stored and mailed out from the new plant.

By then it was a good-sized hike, but Larry Brings walked with pride through the long, carpeted office section on the south side of the building. The computer room, behind its glass wall next to the punch-card room, is almost like a stage overlooking the office area.

The order processors and secretaries have their desks in the large, oblong office. Along the sides are private offices for Lawrence, Keith, Marianne Day, and the editorial and executive staff.

Lawrence has a working office and a "ceremonial office." The working office was piled high with papers and manuscripts, much as in the old days. The ceremonial office, which is only opened for special visitors, is tastefully furnished with many fine pieces from Lawrence's former offices and world travels. The room is dominated by a handsome, massive wood desk with distinctive carvings. Where did he get it? He admitted, with a sheepish grin, that it was the desk from his former office on Fifth Avenue South. "There was always so much stuff on it," he explained. "Nobody could see it." It was the first piece of office furniture he had purchased forty years ago.

Lawrence Brings was born at eight o'clock in the morning, and that's when he always gets to work, and many days earlier. When I took a publications job at Denison last winter, I had the opportunity to see him in action—and I do mean action! That experience stimulated me to write this book, more certainly than any previous association with him. It gave me access to his files and provided me with a detailed picture of his personality, habits and working attitudes.

Everybody at Denison agrees that Mr. Brings chews up work like a meat grinder, with his mind on a dozen things at once. He is often interrupted by phone calls, inquiries from authors, questions about printing jobs, and every variety of business. When visitors come, he escorts them on tours of the plant.

Lawrence Brings is so busy during the regular working week that he goes to the office on Saturday mornings, so he can take care of his private correspondence in peace. He sometimes returns to the plant in the evening, and so does Keith. Forty-hour weeks are not long enough for the people who carry the heavy responsibilities of a business organization.

I learned that Lawrence Brings has not changed his business philosophy. He says he likes to run "a tight ship"—economizing on everything from paper clips to stationery—because it became a lifetime habit during the old days of "hard times." It still bothers him to see anyone wasting good supplies or precious time. He always told his new employees that he wouldn't ask them to do anything he hasn't done, or anything he can't do right now—and maybe quite a bit faster. He is an "efficiency expert" about the proper use of human energy. If someone is making too many awkward motions to get a job done, he demonstrates graceful shortcuts.

Many of the Denison faces were familiar to me, as an author who had popped in and out. Now I had a chance to know them as friends, eating lunch with girls from the office and mailing departments and discussing our mutual interests.

I had written a book called *Ecology for Young People,* which was being published about the same time as my Carl Rowan biography. It was exciting to be on the scene, discussing the art work and illustrations for the ecology book with artist Eddie Olderen who directs the art department in the southeast corner of the building—and hearing about the orders for my new books as they came in. Those wonderful friends took a personal interest in my book-writing career.

"Visitors are surprised to see our employees smile, when they visit our company," Lawrence Brings said with obvious pride. It isn't because they are paid to smile, but they seem to be naturally friendly people. Or they might feel in good spirits from listening to the merry whistling tunes of Ed McGulpin who presides over the mailing department. From the top down, all the people at T. S. Denison and Company are personalities in their own right.

Lawrence Brings has arranged for housewives to get a change of scenery and earn some extra money —without neglecting their families. There are many young mothers who come to work at 9 a.m., after they get their children off to school. They leave the plant at 3 p.m., in time to welcome their youngsters home again.

A spirit of camaraderie and loyalty is apparent in the plant. The work is not easy, but everyone seems to take satisfaction in being part of a smooth operation. From the lively conversations in the lunchroom, punctuated by giggles and laughter, it is obvious that a "resident psychiatrist" is not necessary at T. S. Denison.

Nettie's young sister, Helen Clark, heads the book order department, and her nephew, Dan Clark, is employed in the shipping section. The Brings businesses have always been a family enterprise, and Nettie often comes to the office to help out. "I enjoy working with my little sister," she told me.

It was fun to visit with Nettie during "lunch breaks." She has no ambitions to be a speechmaker, but her sense of humor has made her a captivating storyteller. She and Lawrence have done quite a bit of traveling and wherever they have gone, something hilarious or dramatic has happened.

Trust Nettie to get mixed up with a "Sheik of Araby" on their honeymoon trip around the world.

She might have titled that story, "A Funny Thing Happened to Me on the Way to the Pyramids"—a comedy of errors that would never cease to amuse Larry.

All the tourists were expected to ride on camels. In an exotic blending of East and West, Nettie's camel was named "Queen of Sheba," and Larry's was named "Hi Ho, Silver!"

Nettie found it fairly easy to get aboard her "ship of the desert" while the beast was kneeling, but then the Queen started ascending at a dangerous angle— up-up-up, mostly backside first—swaying from side to side in the process. Balancing precariously and uttering little shrieks, Nettie was certain she would take a nose-dive into the desert sand before the Queen finished her skyward ascension. According to the timid passenger, "It was a terribly tall camel, with such long, spindly legs!"

Torn between laughter and anxiety, her fellow-tourists kept yelling, "Lean back, Nettie! Lean back, Mrs. Brings!"

It took a lot of leaning, but she was finally aloft and feeling fairly secure. All the other members of the group were on their camels, with a walking escort leading each animal. "Hi Ho, Silver"—and away to the pyramids!

Nettie's camel seemed to be stalled, and she suddenly realized that a strange hand was patting her leg. Peering down, she was startled to see her burnoose-draped Egyptian guide taking such liberties— and she had barely met him. What kind of a sheik was this, crouching on the far side of her camel, patting away at her leg?

Nettie stared down at him with a thousand mixed emotions. Was he trying to be a Rudolph Valentino? Then she learned he was interested in her money— not her charms! He wanted some extra money urgently, right then, while the "boss" couldn't see him collecting a secret bonus.

"Wait until the end of the trip," she told him, suddenly noticing in panic that he was detouring her away from the rest of the "camel caravan."

"No, no! The boss will see," he told her. "Money now, now!"

Alarmed that he was going to lead her away into the desert, Nettie signaled her companions in desperation — and her Bedouin boyfriend reluctantly guided the Queen of Sheba into formation with the other camels.

Under her breath Nettie told the other Americans about her difficulties with the greedy guide, and they shared her indignation. At the end of the trip, with Nettie safely on the ground again, they complained to the "boss." When he shrugged their accusations aside with a sly grin, they realized that he was "in cahoots" with any successful extortionists in his camel crew.

There were other adventures in faraway lands. An appointment in New Delhi was more glamorous because of confusion about a street address. Mr. and Mrs. Brings had been invited to visit the home of Dr. Sarvipalli Radhakrishnan, who was Vice President of India in 1961 and would become President the following year.

After making inquiries about the address at their hotel, Larry and Nettie set out in a taxi. Bewildered for awhile, the taxi driver at last located a handsome residence with the appropriate number on the wall beside the gate. They went up a splendid circular driveway and were met at the front entrance by a white-robed servant who bowed and escorted them through spacious rooms to a large formal patio garden at the rear.

There sat a distinguished-looking elderly man, sipping a cool drink. He bowed graciously and welcomed them, apologizing because arthritis made it difficult for him to arise.

He waved them to seats and asked what they would like to drink. While he was clapping for a servant and inquiring whether they wanted soda or lemon, Lawrence started the conversation. "Did you go to Oxford?" he asked.

"No, I was a Cambridge man," his host told him.

"You probably are busy in Parliament at this time of the year," his visitor suggested.

"Oh no, I haven't been in Parliament for thirty-five years!"

Larry and Nettie almost choked on their cocktails. This man was supposed to be the Vice President of India!

"Aren't you Dr. Radhakrishnan?" Lawrence asked in consternation. "Have we come to the wrong house?"

When their accidental host learned they had a 7:30 appointment with the Vice President and were already late, he said, "Oh, he must not be kept waiting!" He was so disturbed that he arose and escorted them to the door, in spite of his infirmities. An explanation by phone was sent immediately to the residence of Dr. Radhakrishnan, and Mr. and Mrs. Brings soon arrived at their intended destination—breathless but thrilled about their chance meeting with a charming stranger who had acted as though he expected them to drop in. Later they learned that he was the son of a former maharaja of India.

Their visit with the real Dr. Radhakrishnan was enlightening. Warmhearted Nettie was worried about the nutrition problems in India and felt compelled to ask about remedies.

When there was a famine in India, Dr. Radhakrishnan told her, international politics sometimes entered the picture and were considered more important than providing food for starving people. In 1953, when the United States had a surplus of wheat, India asked President Eisenhower for some of the excess bounty. The American President said the request would have to be approved by Congress, and of course that would take time. There was a possibility that the appeal might even be denied—for complicated economic reasons. When India turned to the Russians for help, they sent the needed wheat immediately.

There is a brighter side to that story. The United States has often been first in rushing food to famine-stricken areas of India—in 1967, for instance. A certain amount of caution is sometimes necessary to keep from upsetting delicate international trade balances. That coldblooded fact of life is disconcerting to Nettie—and many of the rest of us.

In a *Minneapolis Star* interview after they returned home, Lawrence noted that the Russians were quick to capitalize on the world's desires—whether it was wheat for India or the Aswan Dam for Egypt. In 1961, he was "shocked by the intensity of Soviet determination to have a Communist world." At that time, Russia and China were placing "prime emphasis on infiltration rather than direct military conquest."

Lawrence was scheduled to describe his trip at his Rotary Club luncheon—and as a result he later addressed fifty different organizations on "The Menace of Communism."

Nettie keeps running into "dramatic happenings" wherever they go. When they were in Florida last winter, Lawrence and Nettie set out on a cruise to the West Indies. There was a fire aboard the ship, but Nettie has no hilarious memories of that experience. She is still petrified.

Until I saw Lawrence Brings getting ready to go to Florida last December, I had thought of it mainly as a *vacation* for him. My view from inside the office was quite different. During the week before he and Nettie were scheduled to leave, he kept assembling empty boxes and filling them full of business papers, correspondence, manuscripts and a variety of reading and working material from his desk and files. It was an impressive sight! Suddenly I realized that he does not leave the office—he takes it with him.

Even when he goes home from the office in the afternoon, he always takes a bulging briefcase with him to study the contents while he's watching television. It is difficult to know how many things are going on in his mind simultaneously, but an observer can see that he is always doing more than one thing at a time.

One day, when I was querying him about some research material, he was opening a large stack of letters. He and Keith usually open all the T. S. Denison mail, I learned. I watched in fascination as LMB slit the envelopes open with one swift motion, scanned the contents with speed-reading efficiency, made notations on each one, and filed the orders, letters and checks in convenient pigeonholes. At the same time he was carrying on a perfectly lucid conversation with me. "How can you do all those things at once?" I finally blurted out.

"Oh, this is nothing," he answered. "When I'm at home, I often examine manuscripts and watch television at the same time—while Nettie is talking to me. She says I'm not listening to her, but I am!"

Larry Brings has trained himself to save time by doubling up on his work load. His good friend, Clifford Sommer, recently asked if he still reads books while driving a car. Then I remembered hearing LMB mention, years ago, that he had read one of my manuscripts while he was driving to Duluth. Some people merely drive, and they are the ones who have accidents.

T. S. Denison now has a brilliant and charming new editor, Willard E. Rosenfelt, who reads manuscripts and advises authors, although Lawrence Brings still keeps an eye on any prospective publications.

Usually Marianne Day answers all the questions and knows where to track down anything in the long row of files in the main office. Sometimes customers send vague descriptions of plays that were published twenty or thirty years ago, and it should be remembered that there were thousands of them in a multitude of catalogs. Even with the flimsiest of clues, Marianne can remember the name of the play and the catalog listing.

Now that everything is computerized, the girls must be nimble-witted about punchcard numbers as well as titles. You can look around the sparkling new plant, comparing its technological advances with the old one, and feel the urge to say, "Lawrence M. Brings has come a *long* way!"

Chapter Eighteen

"What God Hath Wrought"

The epic drama of Central Lutheran Church has been a "continued story," a miracle play in the modern tradition. With its strong spiritual, human and financial foundation, it promises to endure as a fortress of faith.

In 1969, Central Lutheran celebrated its Fiftieth Birthday with all its candles of "service to others" gleaming brightly.

This announcement about *What God Hath Wrought* received headline prominence in the Central publication, *Spirit of Central:* "Brings Chronicles Central's 50 Years." The congregation learned that a tremendous research and writing project had been undertaken and completed. No finer book review could have been written than the following testimonial:

"Perhaps the most significant event of Central's 50th anniversary is the publication of the history of Central, *What God Hath Wrought,*" by Lawrence M. Brings. This 240-page history, replete with pertinent illustrations, will not only delight the members of the congregation but will give valuable insights into the problems, the challenges and the role of a large inner city congregation in the changing city. In a day in which the life and role of inner city churches are being reexamined, this book will be read with great interest by pastors and congregations who are involved in similar settings in the American city.

"One could scarcely find a more qualified author to handle the story of Central. Besides being an author and publisher himself, Mr. Brings has served as general superintendent of the Sunday School for 15 years, chairman of the Fireside Hour for seven years, and chairman of the board of trustees for 26 years. He has served continuously as chairman of the board of the Central Lutheran Foundation . . ."

Since this biographer identified the "mystery man" by the clues in *What God Hath Wrought,* it seems that the secret has been kept for long enough. Obviously Lawrence Brings did save Central by "safeguarding" the bonds that might have driven the church into bankruptcy, but why was he so modest about his good works?

Perhaps some indications might be found in the meaningful subtitles in *What God Hath Wrought.* Here Lawrence Brings exulted in scholarship, with quotations from the Bible and the classics. The following are typical:

> "To God alone the glory."
> "This is the Lord's doing.
>   It is marvelous in our eyes."
> "If God be with us, who can be against us?"

In those three subtitles, he sounded as though he were not working alone. He was crediting the power of "divine assistance." In another quotation, from Robinson Jeffers, he expressed the philosophy he shared with the original founders of Central Lutheran Church:

"Lend me the stone strength of the past,
And I will lend you the wings of the future."

The wings of his imagination had carried Lawrence Brings upward and onward, but "the stone strength" of Little Canada had provided the discipline to make success possible.

Readers of the book would gasp at the incredible number of organizations and projects that the church had sponsored, almost from the beginning. A few of them were mentioned in that issue of *Spirit of Central.*

One of the high points of that Fiftieth Anniversary celebration was the lofty new total in the Central Lutheran Foundation Fund. Lawrence announced it on page 179 of *What God Hath Wrought:* "At the time of this writing, the Foundation assets exceeded $850,000." That was in April, 1969. By 1973 it had passed the million mark.

Naturally the Foundation fund did not stop growing. To modern radicals who denounce "materialism," its blending of dollars with divinity might seem a contradiction—but that money seems to have produced an expansive feeling of spiritual health and well-being. Living with poverty can be much more painful; it pinches the soul.

Almost four years have been added to the history of Central Lutheran since its Fiftieth Anniversary, and its watchword is still "Forward"—in the congregation, in the community, in the city and the world. Lawrence Brings is not standing still. As an authority on setting up Foundations, he continues to serve as an unpaid consultant to a variety of church and educational groups.

Because of his activities on behalf of Central Lutheran and his many philanthropic good deeds, Lawrence Brings is recognized as a friend by other great men and community leaders.

Clifford C. Sommer, who did not want LMB to move to Chicago in 1950, knew Larry as a fellow-member of Central Lutheran back in the middle 1930s. They had become kindred souls in their visions of a Greater Central when Lawrence was chairman of the Board of Trustees and Clifford was a member of the Board in 1948. Agreeing that Central would need to expand, they had their eyes on some adjoining residential property that might be purchased with little difficulty. With a congregation of 5,000 by that time, the cost per member would be minimal.

Every time the board met, Clifford Sommer would introduce a motion to buy that property as soon as it became available. As Chairman, Lawrence could not second the motion—and they waited in vain for someone else to do it. "I don't know how many times we waited for somebody to second that motion," Clifford Sommer declared recently. "Maybe it was only six times, but it might have been twelve or thirteen!"

At last someone on the board made this obvious statement, "We know you and Larry want to buy that property. It would be a good investment, but that is not what is bothering us. We'll consider buying it—if you'll agree not to build on it right away!" They didn't start building immediately, according to Clifford Sommer. They waited a whole six months!

Mr. Sommer is a man who can appreciate the leadership qualities of other men who devote time to worthwhile goals, instead of being content merely to earn a living for themselves and operate in narrow, cramped circles of self-interest. In addition to a multitude of other activities, Mr. Sommer was President of the American Bankers Association during 1971—the first and only Minnesotan to be chosen for that lofty national honor.

It was a pleasure to visit Clifford Sommer in his handsome office on the twelfth floor of the Northwestern National Bank in Minneapolis and hear about the years when he was summoned to Owatonna, Minnesota, to serve as President and Director of the famous Security Bank and Trust Company.

While they were living in Minneapolis, it had been necessary to drive four miles to Central Lutheran Church. Mr. Sommer was an usher who sometimes had to be on duty for more than one service, and he had wondered if it might have been a hardship for his wife and daughters to take the bus home when he couldn't accompany them. Evidently it hadn't. After they had lived in Owatonna for awhile, he asked them, "Is there anything you miss from our old lives in Minneapolis?"

"There is one thing," they told him. "Central Lutheran Church!"

He still marvels at the glow of significance that Central Lutheran sheds on the lives of the congregation—inspiring eagerness to participate wholeheartedly in its services, organizations, and spiritual "life style."

That is why he is enthusiastic about an inner city church called Central Lutheran. Because Central is "so large in scope," it attracts a variety of interesting people from outside the core area, as well as those who live nearby. That, he feels, is a healthy situation because it helps to keep the inner city alive and pulsing with permanent activity.

Clifford Sommer is looking forward to Larry Brings' company on another fund-raising campaign in the near future. Mr. Sommer has had some experience of his own in promoting fund-raising drives for good works and worthwhile purposes. Without divulging any of their secrets, it might be said that they are successful because their technique is never haphazard. It is carefully planned and based on strategy that appeals to the benevolent natures of prospective contributors.

Speaking of fund-raising, how about those bond-holders who felt compelled to sell their bonds at a large discount after the Depression? Did Mr. Sommer think they carried grudges? A few might have, but it is possible that most of them have looked at Central Lutheran Church and have felt gratified because they, too, helped to rescue it from disaster. Blessings come in many disguises.

Above all, Clifford Sommer agreed, it was a blessing that Lawrence Brings was a dedicated member of Central Lutheran at such a tense period in history, and that he was vigilant about avoiding a similar threat—far into the years of prosperity and good times.

No matter how awesome the challenge, Lawrence Brings has always possessed a talent for "putting everything together, for grasping the whole picture without wasting time." He could be described as "a professional about money"—but Clifford Sommer had observed that Lawrence Brings' active, fertile brain held much more than images of pennies and dollars. He had an intellectual background, with imagination and a sense of history to widen his perspective. We must remember that he was reciting entire plays by Shakespeare, George Bernard Shaw, and other classicists—hundreds and hundreds of times. In his mind is a powerful reservoir of human understanding as seen through the eyes of philosophers and religious scholars.

As Clifford Sommer so aptly summed it up, "He has knowledge, and knowledge is power. When a man pours that power into worthwhile endeavors, as Larry Brings does, it is an unbeatable combination."

As a dramatist, Lawrence Brings' sense of "timing" had usually been perfect—and that talent carried over into his fund-raising activities. Philanthropic programs have been as important to him as promoting his own private business. He used the same system for both of them. He has always been "imaginative" about money.

The Central Lutheran Church Foundation, born so humbly in the shadows of the Great Depression, now exceeds one million dollars. In addition to Lawrence Brings' personal solicitations and campaign leadership, Mr. Sommer noted, the Foundation has profited from annual church collections in honor of Dr. Stub's memory and other voluntary memorial gifts. It has become a healthy spiritual habit—to "lay up heavenly treasures" on earth.

Another of Larry Brings' long-time friends and admirers, Esther Gehrke, served as Chairman of the Official History Committee for the Fiftieth Anniversary of Central Lutheran Church. As a Charter Member, she was there during the founding years. "I remember the growing years—the painful years!" Esther exclaimed, her voice bubbling with good cheer. Perhaps her attitude is a clue to Central's success. It owes its survival to members who could endure challenges and hardships — and emerge in triumph. They do not try to sound "religious," but they have the spiritual invincibility of Daniel in the lion's den.

Esther recalls Lawrence Brings as the young speech professor whose school was located in Minneapolis. In those postwar, Warren G. Harding years, the younger generation was trying to get a foothold in the business world. It was especially commendable that a small urban congregation worked with equal vigor to help their new church get ahead. Both Clifford Sommer and Esther Gehrke were astonished that Central Lutheran had grown from twelve small families with "a vision of service" in 1919 to a large congregation with a magnificent new church in 1926.

Since Esther was familiar with the church history and records, Lawrence Brings asked her for information when he was compiling and writing *What God Hath Wrought,* the story of Central's first fifty years. Much of the research material was assembled by T. S. Denison author Dr. L. E. Leipold and sent to Lawrence while he was in Florida—presumably "vacationing" in a warmer climate, but still working longer hours than anybody. The history of Central Lutheran Church was close to his heart, and he was anxious to get all the details straight.

"We had to dig through boxes and boxes of old records, searching for membership lists and cradle rolls, and looking for the dates when organizations were formed—and all the human interest stories that might appeal to modern readers," Esther said. Some of the most appealing would be notices of full-course dinners, served by the church ladies, for thirty-five and fifty cents. Multitudes of money-raising and money-saving activities have been promoted within Central Lutheran over the years, all bearing some resemblance to the Gospel story about the "loaves and fishes."

Esther Gehrke is thrilled that the Foundation assets have grown from $850,000 to one million dollars since the publication of *What God Hath Wrought.* Although the principal is not touched, the Foundation was able to secure control of the old debt on the sanctuary—which is now debt free. According to the book, "It also made loans to the congregation, which led to the construction of the parish house, purchases of parking lots, financing the chancel remodeling and securing the new Cassavant organ. This program of support is to be continued in the future."

For Central, it was almost like owning its own bank! Esther Gehrke noted that the Foundation fund has paid $555,000 in earnings to the congregation since its founding. "The principal cannot be touched," she declared. "The Foundation is set up that way, so the church will never be in a 'money-tight' position again. We older people remember all those years of anxiety. Some of the younger people have ideas about spending some of that Foundation million. It looks easy to them, knowing that all that money is there, but the Foundation is a separate corporate entity with a self-perpetuating board of trustees and the congregation has no authority to alter its fiscal policy.

It looks as though that million dollars is in the same class as The Rock of Ages—and just as invulnerable now!

Chapter Nineteen

Working for Fun

The reader must have gathered, by now, that the subject of this biography is a very contradictory gentleman. If you study him as a businessman, you might envy or disapprove of his talents for pulling off smart business transactions—and feeling triumphant about them.

LMB has often cast himself perfectly in the role of the shrewd, hardnosed businessman who cares about making a profit. Undoubtedly some of his authors have viewed him that way—as something of a Scrooge when their royalty checks turn out puny.

Then there is another Lawrence Brings — the philanthropist who works with prodigious energy for the profit and welfare of other people. Here he has often played his role behind the scenes, as the "mysterious stranger" who saved Central Lutheran Church and as a member of exclusive leadership councils promoting fund-raising drives for worthwhile causes and projects.

Many organizations, including the YMCA, have profited from Larry's voluntary promotional work.

He has served as a board member of the Union City Mission and Goodwill Industries, in addition to all his Foundation activities.

Fifteen years ago, as a member of the executive committee and vice president, he helped to spearhead the $17,000,000 Minneapolis Hospital Fund Drive. Recently he announced the grand and glorious conclusion of that campaign. Each hospital received its allotted share. A balance of $170,000 in interest had accumulated over the years, and it was divided up among the hospitals. That kind of interest is dear to the heart of Lawrence Brings. All you do is save, and there it is!

As a member and treasurer of the Board of Regents of Golden Valley Lutheran College, Lawrence Brings has been promoting the establishment of a Foundation there. Here, there, and everywhere! At the risk of becoming dizzy from so much "Big Money Talk," we are listing Lawrence's activities at the end of the book. Wherever he has presided or officiated, it can be safely assumed that he has accelerated building programs and increased the financial reserves of the organizations.

Whether he worked as Superintendent of the Central Lutheran Sunday School for fifteen years, or as President of the Central Lutheran and Minnesota Protestant Foundations, he cared about leaving his "hobbies and avocations" in much better shape than he found them. They are the beneficiaries of his generosity and unselfish contributions of time and energy.

Among his many roles is Lawrence Brings, the traveler, who knows when to spend money and enjoy it. It's more economical to stay at home and eat at home, but he enjoys getting out into the world and meeting people. Whether it is thrifty or not, he considers an occasional change of scenery as invigorating as a tonic.

Some of Lawrence Brings' letters seem quite funny in retrospect. More than ten years ago, he wrote that he and Mrs. Brings planned to take a two-weeks' cruise from New York to the West Indies. It had been a long, cold winter in Minneapolis, and he added, "I find it necessary for me to curtail my tense procedures here if I am to keep up the busy schedule I maintain. At my age, I suppose that it is doubly necessary for me to watch that I keep up good mental and physical attitudes."

After a long, hectic life of coaching speech students at five in the morning, getting to the office by eight, and often working far past midnight, his intuition must have told him he was reaching the normal age for retirement. Many of his contemporaries were looking forward to sleeping late and finding a sunny place to loll on the sidelines.

Looking at Lawrence Brings now—still hurrying into the office every morning at the age of seventy-five—it is obvious that he doesn't pay much attention to his intuition. Not where work is concerned. In a world where "dirty little four-letter words" are too fashionable, he wishes that *work* would become popular again.

He can look back to the age of the horse and buggy and remember the cycles in modern history when the fruits of labor meant prosperity for the country—and self-respect for everyone who worked.

Lawrence Brings has no fond memories of the years of unemployment and the Depression. He does not feel that work can cure everything, but he thinks it's about the best remedy the Good Lord ever invented.

Lawrence Brings, the worker, is another contradiction. Through his own industry and economical practices, LMB managed to put an adequate sum into annuities. When he married Ethel, they decided always to invest 50% of their income, a practice they continued for many years. For almost fifteen years after the publishing company was started, neither Lawrence nor his wife drew any compensation. The profits were used to expand the business. For the past ten years, he has been working without a salary as a businessman. The man who comes to his office at T. S. Denison every morning, scoots through the various departments to check operations, and gobbles up more work than several normal individuals —this man does not draw a salary. He is living on the interest from his annuities and his trust fund, a pattern that he established for the Central Lutheran Foundation.

At a time when many "humanitarian idealists" are demanding higher salaries for themselves, it might seem strange for a practical businessman to keep putting his heart and energy into the publishing organization he founded—without taking anything out of it. He believes that as the editor who selects manuscripts now, as he has done for over forty-five years, he can make a contribution to the improvement of educational books.

Perhaps that is the key to all these mental meanderings. This is "the publishing organization he founded"—one of the two highest crests in his never-dull life. Saving Central, and keeping it saved, is the other.

The T. S. Denison enterprises are not to be taken lightly by Lawrence Brings, in fair weather or foul. Right now is a low time for the book business, as most publishers know. In the East, famous old publishing houses have been merging to cut costs and remain afloat somehow. It seems as if the publishing business is holding its breath, waiting for substantial appropriations to return.

If you listen to him and observe his occasional moments of anxiety, you will understand that he is now trying to "save" T. S. Denison and its expensive new plant—in much the same way that he worked furiously to save Central Lutheran Church three decades ago. This is no small feat for a man of seventy-five who has already accepted a multitude of challenges in his life. He is straining to keep the company from moving backward, until the present "publishing recession" has run its course. In this, he and his son have been successful in operating with a balance in the black each year.

This is not the first time Lawrence Brings has faced handicaps and disappointments. He has always tried to be optimistic—accepting the inevitable and turning it into a triumph. How can he relax when he knows there is still another battle to be fought, another crest that demands to be climbed? Here is the most precarious climax of them all, when most men would be least prepared to "try, try again!"

Newspapers, magazines, and book publishing companies have failed in recent years. Will T. S. Denison weather this Great Publishing Depression? We are betting on Lawrence Brings to survive— because he has always practiced thrift and knows when to cut back on operational expenses. When it comes to money, his favorite answer is "No."

This man can be irritating at times, but he is never mundane. His humor is quick and smooth, making light of human frailties and frustrations, and he brings out the wit in other people. Soon the disgruntled author or employee is chuckling with him, ready to go back to work after blowing off steam.

The people who are close to Lawrence Brings realize that he has more reason to feel frustrated than anyone. He is operating differently now, and the metamorphosis has to be experienced to be understood. During the more prosperous 1960s, authors were writing under the stress of continuous deadlines, and new books were streaming off the busy T. S. Denison presses. Now authors are complaining about procrastination, while they wait for a year or two for their books to be published.

When business is poor and printing costs are inflated, everybody suffers. Printers and typesetters are laid off. Publishers hesitate to gamble on books that might take too long to absorb their printing and advertising costs, before they begin to show a profit. They want a "guaranteed assurance" that a new textbook or biography won't languish on the storage shelves. New literature must quickly prove itself a "staple commodity"—like pork and beans. That is not a healthy intellectual situation, and it makes Lawrence Brings restless and uncomfortable. He is too accustomed to rushing ahead, achieving, accomplishing, and marking his path with publishing milestones that he can see and count.

Even as he strives to maintain T. S. Denison with its old vigor, Lawrence Brings keeps his youthful resiliency in a changing world. He loves books, but he recognizes that they might eventually become as obsolete as the cuneiform inscriptions of the ancient Sumerians. "Tapes and films," he predicted recently, "will be the major teaching aids of the future. Educational writers will have to change their techniques." He is already far ahead of them in evaluating the atmosphere of the Twenty-first Century classroom.

As a modern book publisher, Larry Brings is probably the greatest contradiction of them all. While opposing sex and profanity in the books he publishes, LMB has always been open-minded about editorial innovations and new approaches to current history. In the last chapters of my Henry Luce and Carl Rowan biographies, I "dared to editorialize" about some conclusions I had reached while gathering information for those books. If I wanted to start a new trend in the handling of biographies, it was all right with Lawrence Brings. Any form of new enlightenment appeals to him, especially if it has been ignored by the communications media and other publishers.

That type of "freedom of expression" is often more important to an author than this moment's fame and fortune. We are glad that our points of view are "on the record" in libraries, to help counter-balance the tons of sensationalism, radicalism and sheer pornography on the other side of the scale. We like to feel that we are expressing the indignation of almost two hundred million normal Americans who do not share the sentiments of publishers and commentators who have glorified hippies, drugs and sexual freedom. Come to think of it, all the T. S. Denison authors could be described as "normal people," speaking for the people they know best.

In addition to his editorial endeavors, the versatility of LMB is apparent on any working day. He gives the office mail his speedy personal attention, distributing it to the proper people for processing. He might pause long enough to answer a question —before he darts back to his office desk or out to the printing department to check on the progress of a job. Ten minutes later, you might see him conferring with an author, customer or salesman in the office area of the reception room. On the way back to his office, he picks up speed to take a phone call, of which he has many.

The Brings perpetual motion program includes conducting tours through the entire plant for interested visitors. Whether he is playing the gracious host, the T. S. Denison editor, the shrewd business-man, or performing any of a dozen minor duties, he is a whole cast of characters in a play entitled "T. S. Denison and Company." Remember when he acted all the roles in those dramatic readings, many long years ago?

Lawrence's speech and entertainment books continue to sell well, but the once-proud collection of

T. S. Denison plays has been relegated to a small section of pigeonholes at the rear of the order department. The spooky melodramas have become true ghost stories now, haunting reminders of Tom Denison and his first small publishing company in Chicago more than a century ago.

Memories of the past are still important to Lawrence Brings. He has kept some fascinating Chicago newspaper clippings, dating back to the years before he ever guessed that he and T. S. Denison might become "synonymous."

In the same spirit, Larry enjoys reviving old friendships and revisiting scenes that are worth remembering. In 1946 he was an honored guest at the high school senior class reunion at New Richmond, Wisconsin. In 1971 he and Nettie were invited to the Fiftieth Anniversary of the same senior class. It was a time to recall the first teaching goals of an energetic young graduate fresh out of Gustavus Adolphus.

After that festive occasion in 1971, Lawrence said he was startled to see that there were so many "senior citizens" in the Class of 1921. Even though they were only a few years younger than he, it seemed as though he should be looking into the faces of those "high-spirited kids" again. The years had passed so quickly without his realizing that he, too, was no longer so young. Listening to him, it was apparent that he was not yet in the mood to be a "senior citizen."

Naturally Nettie Brings became involved in all of Lawrence's activities, sharing his memories with the understanding and charm that are typical of her personality. Her sparkling conversation and wit are welcome everywhere — at the Denison plant, at church and social gatherings, and any place where people appreciate a delightful lady who is "extra special." It is obvious that Lawrence appreciates her very much.

Nobody has forgotten that it was Keith and Barbara, and the daughter in the Johnson family, who brought Nettie and Lawrence together. It was the reverse of "Bless you, my children!"

When Nettie talks about her sons she refers to them as "Bill" and "Jim," in spite of their distinguished degrees and titles. The older son, William R. Johnson, has a lifetime appointment as a Superior Court Judge in New Hampshire. He is the one who was graduated from Dartmouth. Then he received his law degree from Harvard.

James C. Johnson, whose graduation exercises Lawrence attended with Nettie at the University of Arizona in 1966, returned to Arizona for his Master's Degree and later received his Doctor's Degree from the University of Minnesota. Dr. Johnson is now a professor in the Department of Marketing and Management at the University of Tulsa.

Not to be outdone by her brothers, Nettie's daughter was graduated from the University of Minnesota with a major in psychology. After her marriage to Emil Souba, Patricia went back to college in Sioux Falls, South Dakota, and is qualified as a certified social service worker.

Nettie has often talked informally about her family. It was Lawrence who gave me all these particulars, efficiently, concisely, and all on the spur of the moment. "Wasn't Judge William quite young for a lifetime appointment?" I asked.

"Yes," he agreed proudly. "He's only about forty-three." His feeling of kinship with Nettie's family is a pleasing trait.

He had already spoken at length of his admiration and affection for Keith as the son who was quietly shouldering the responsibility for the complicated operation of T. S. Denison and its affiliates. Lawrence knew that he could depend on Keith whenever he went to Florida for the cold winter months and on trips to faraway places.

Keith, too, is trying to build T. S. Denison, experimenting with new sales techniques and other innovations. Keith has worked his way up in the organization, never expecting special favors as the "Big Boss' son." He takes an interest in the entire plant, just as his father does, and he can often be seen pounding out letters at a desk in the main office—just like the other employees. Unassuming, conscientious, and almost too calm in appearance, Keith is likely to inspire this question, "What is really going on in his mind?"

On rare occasions Barbara Brings visits the office, perhaps with one of the children. She is still the attractive blonde girl, the glamorous daughter of playwright Robert St. Clair. Keith and Barbara have two sons and a daughter. Their grandfather's face glows with pleasure as he talks of their interests and talents:

"Sherrie is a senior at Breck School. She worked with retarded children four years and plans to become a teacher of special education. Kent, who is fifteen, is the athlete in the family. Todd, at thirteen, seems most likely to carry on the family theatrical traditions. 'He's the actor!' " Lawrence grinned. Both Kent and Todd are students at Blake School.

It remains to be seen whether any of the grandchildren will choose to enter the publishing business. Their grandfather will surely advise them about its pleasures and pitfalls. He would not want them to serve an "apprenticeship" in a truck garden or fight their way through howling blizzards for a chance to go to high school. Yet, when we look back through his seventy-five years of filling each day to its utmost capacity, it is evident that the hardships of his childhood were more of a blessing than a punishment. At any rate, he survived them for three-quarters of a century — and still has the youthful spirit and ambition of a man half his age.

Perhaps that is the secret of a successful life, to fill the years with new hopes and ambitions, new crests to climb. His latest ambition is to expand the Denison publishing program. He does not appear fainthearted about this newest challenge to his ingenuity. It keeps him on his toes, as though life is a test of willpower and fortitude. Lawrence Brings simply refuses to be feeble and weary, when there are so many worthwhile jobs to be tackled.

To authors, publishers are men of prestige and awesome power. When a manuscript is mailed to one of them, an author might wonder, "What kind of a man is this publisher? Will he deal kindly with my brainchild—waving his magic wand and turning it into a book? Will he actually read it, and will he understand the creative urges and frustrations that went into its composition?"

Lawrence Brings does read manuscripts, and he would be the first to understand creative urges and frustrations because they gave him the momentum to become a leading book publisher, a trainer of hundreds of articulate speakers, and a financial genius who could save a church from bankruptcy and established handsomely funded foundations.

People who know of Lawrence Brings' humble beginnings and look today at the spacious new T. S. Denison publishing plant are likely to exclaim, "He certainly has come up in the world!" Now, when he most deserves to relax, he is still moving forward and upward. Recently he said, "I don't think we should be going to Florida this winter. There is so much work to do here!"

That does not mean he will spend all his time in Minneapolis. After he exhibited books at the Minnesota Educational Association Convention, he was off to New Jersey, Oklahoma, California and a number of other states for similar conventions.

Lawrence has just renewed his passport. "Keith tells me I should travel while I can," he confided, one Saturday morning recently—talking and opening three huge stacks of mail at the same time, as usual.

Behind him was the thrill of a lifetime. The Central Lutheran Choir sang in Bethlehem on Christmas Eve, 1972, and Lawrence and Nettie were there. What could be better than this? To live with hard work and devotion to duty—and earn the right to participate in sublime moments of history!

Lawrence Brings keeps saying that he is "slowing down" on his working schedule, but he admitted that he often wakes up at 5:30 in the morning and eats a light breakfast. He takes a sandwich to the plant for his noon lunch and sometimes spends only ten or fifteen minutes in the lunchroom. "I do look forward to a good dinner at night!" he said. "There is one difference in my habits, now that I am trying to take it easier. I go to bed earlier."

Theatergoing, for pleasure as well as professional research, was once a thrilling activity in his life. Which does he prefer now—the Guthrie or TV? He enjoys attending the Guthrie occasionally. As for television dramas, most of them seem "old-hat" to him. The plots have become too familiar. "Sometimes I even get bored with 'All in the Family,' " he said of that top-rated program. He always watches the news, of course, and he appreciated the "real life drama" of the political conventions and the Olympics. But you won't find him staying awake for the late shows—not when there is so much work to be done in the daytime. He hopes that he will live to help celebrate the centennial of the company in 1976.

There are always large and small jobs awaiting the Minneapolis publisher who has disciplined himself to do anything that anybody can do—and quite a bit more, quite a bit faster.

His ethical standards have been an inspiration to many hard-working authors who care deeply about his survival as a publisher—not so much from a monetary point of view but because there are so few leading publishers who perpetuate the splendid, solid values of this "sweet land of liberty" where

"Faith of Our Fathers" soars with reverent gusto toward humble ceilings of small churches and vaulted arches of great cathedrals.

Contrary to some nonsensical modern notions, Lawrence Martin Brings will always believe that the Great American Dream is founded on the willingness to *work*. The satisfaction of a good day's work should be viewed with the same respect as faith in God, independence of spirit, and confidence in the free enterprise system. It is this philosophy that enabled a poor boy from a truck farm in Little Canada to become a major book publisher west of the Mississippi.

National Board of Advisory Editors

Frederick W. Hill, Ph.D., Deputy Superintendent of Schools, Hicksville, New York

Mrs. Kathlyn King Lundgren, Library Services Center Director, Scottsbluff, Nebraska

L. Edmond Leipold, Ph.D., Former High School Principal, Minneapolis Public Schools

George D. Spache, Ph.D., Head, Reading Laboratory & Clinic, University of Florida

Bryng Bryngelson, Ph.D., Former Director, Speech & Hearing Dept., University of Minnesota

Roger Johnson, Th.D., Department of Religion, Wellesley College

Board of Directors

The Operating Staff

Keith M. Brings, president and chief executive officer

Lawrence M. Brings, senior editor

W. E. Rosenfelt, associate editor

Donald F. Hill, controller and treasurer

Frank Loritz, production manager

Donald Harrer, assistant production manager

Edward Olderen, director, art department

Edwin McGulpin, manager, mailing division

David Mesich, director of computer services

Marianne Day, office manager

Helen Clark, manager, shipping department

Doris Neuenfeldt, corporate secretary

Richard Schmidt, manager, plant services and warehousing

Church and Civic Activities

American Legion member since 1921

Cooperative Club, District Governor

Coast Guard League, District Governor

Lakeshore Athletic Club, President

Rotary Club, Board of Directors

Lutheran Luncheon Club, President

Minnesota Council of Churches, Board of Directors

Central Lutheran Church Foundation, Founder and President

Minnesota Protestant Foundation, Founder and President

Folke Bernadotte Memorial Foundation, Trustee

Minneapolis Hospital Research Council, Executive Committee

National Thespian Dramatic Society

Republican Party

Minneapolis Civic Council

Minneapolis Society of Fine Arts

Lafayette Club

Pi Kappa Delta Speech Fraternity

Sunday School Superintendent, Central Lutheran Church

Central Lutheran Church Men's Club, President

Young Men's Christian Association, Committee of Management

Greater Gustavus Fund, Board Member

Union City Mission, Board Member

Goodwill Industries, Board Member

Lutheran Bible Institute, Surviving Founder

Minneapolis Aquatennial, Committee Chairman

President's Advisory Committee, Gustavus Adolphus College

Minneapolis Executives, President

Masonic Lodge, Scottish Rite, Shriner

Minneapolis $17,000,000 Hospital Fund Drive, Board Member and Vice President

Golden Valley Lutheran College, Board of Regents and Treasurer

Golden Valley Lutheran College Foundation, President

Campaign Chairman, Third Congressional District Republican Candidate for Congress, Two Terms

Phi Mu Gamma, National Honorary Dramatic Sorority, Honorary Member

Life Member, Greater Gustavus Association

Usadian Club, President

Central Lutheran Church Fireside Hour, Chairman

Student Union Building Fund Campaign, Gustavus Adolphus College, Chairman

Acknowledgment

The author would like to salute the following members of the T. S. Denison and Brings Press "family" who, in one way or another, furnished information for this book; all of whom have contributed to the success of the companies:

Jean Anderson

Leola Ault

Blanche Austin

Viola Bakken

Eileen Bendtsen

Vicky Brevik

Shirley Byron

Robert Carlson

Viola Chaffe

Jerry Chase

Helen Clark

Dan Clark Jr.

Thomas Cram

Carol Dammann

Marianne Day

Donald Hill

James Johnson

Mary Johnson

Maragaretha Knealing

Wilma Leipold

Sharon Leipold

Howard Lindberg

Edwin McGulpin

Naomi Melzer

Betty Menzel

David Mesich

Paul Nelson

Doris Neuenfeldt

Edward Olderen

Richard Olsby

Shirley Pitzrick

June Rengstorff

Emeraldo Rios

Willard Rosenfelt

Craig Schiller

Richard Schmidt

Signe Shaler

Dorothea Sommers

Angela Souba

Catherine Spandl

Greg Spandl

Kathleen Sparrow

Wilma Thompson

Muriel Thorman

Viola Welshons

Delores Werner

Steve Weyer

Robert Adams

Irene Ahl

Muriel Barnard

Roger Berg

Richard Bergman

Harold Burns

Daryl Carlson

Dale Chapin

Mary Crotty

Bernice Dimler

Vernon Everson

Raymond Fashingbauer

Lincoln Flamo

Neil Freeman

Pauline Fritsch

Calvin Garner

Dennis Granau

Steve Grindeland

Donna Harju

Donald Harrer

Lloyd Hedstrom

Delores Heinle

William Huffman

Ralph Johnston

Floyd Joynes

Alvin Kratz

George Lanz

Myra Lebak

Clifford Lehner

Joseph Lemanski

Betty Leonardson

Frank Loritz

John Malinsky

Clifford Mason

Joseph Meagher Jr.

Jerry Olson

Katherine Oszman

Warren Palm

Robert Peterson

Donald Pfalz

Lois Pitkin

Leon Rivers

Gregory Rohow

Gordon Rohrbacher

Keith Rohrbacher

Larry Runkel

June Savik

Donald Sewray

Gary Sewray

James Sturgeon

Myrtle Swanson

Vernon Teichroew

Walter Vodegel

Dennis Webster

Steve Wehman